THE ETERNAL SHTUP

Books by Roy Sanders

GONE
PERFECT PEARLS
GIBSON & CLARKE
THE LAYLA PROJECT
TWIN KINGS
MORTY, The Hippy, Dippy Rabbi
MORTY'S MIRACLE MARIJUANA
ISIS WANTS YOU
DEATH BY CANNOLI
CONSIGLIERE
INMATE 772-541
ACCUSED
DIRECTED VERDICT
THE ETERNAL SHTUP

THE ETERNAL SHTUP

a truly divine comedy

ROY SANDERS

ISBN 978-1-956001-25-9 (paperback)
ISBN 978-1-956001-26-6 (eBook)

Copyright © 2021 by Roy Sanders

All rights reserved. No part of this publication may be reproduced, distributed, or transmitted in any form or by any means, including photocopying, recording, or other electronic or mechanical methods without the prior written permission of the publisher.

Printed in the United States of America

Got zitst oiben un poret unter.
God sits on high and makes matches below
*

Esiz besser a shandeh in ponem aider a vaitik in hartsen
It is better to be embarrassed than heartbroken
*

Popular Yiddish Proverbs

Disclaimer

Obviously this is a work of fiction. I have never been to heaven. Being totally objective, chances are good I may never get there either. Names, characters, places and incidents are a product of the author's fertile and overactive imagination and used fictitiously. Honest to You-Know-Who.

Dedication

*"To all the girls I've loved before
Who traveled in and out my door
I'm glad they came along.
I dedicate this song
To all the girls I've loved before."*

Courtesy of Hal David and Albert Hammond, with a shout out to two great singers, Willie Nelson and Julio Iglesias

On a more serious note, I'd like to acknowledge I have been married a few times, engaged a few other times and had a number of long term, more than 90 day, relationships. Each and every one of them, in some measure, contributed to this book. Some good, some bad. To name names would not only be unfair, but get me in a world of hurt. Thanks for understanding.

The single constant in my semi vagabond existence, my unbelievable, loving and accepting children, Greg and Felicia. I love you both more than words can express.

One last word on the subject. The past is just that. The past. Today I am entering my sixth year, can you believe it, in a most wonderful, most gratifying, most loving long term relationship. Thanks Marti.

Author's Notes

When your family physician begins to recommend you see specialists more often than your dental hygienist, you become concerned. That does not nor should not imply this is the last great novel from my all too fertile brain – far from it. I am getting old. Better make that, getting older. Sounds better. What happens next I began to wonder? Without becoming far too personal, as my few friends, those who still admit to knowing me, will tell you, I have a completely unfounded reputation for enjoying what some would call the fruits of the weaker sex. Not true. All I will admit to is, I have always had a most healthy appetite.

I wondered, on the off chance I ended up UP THERE, what my chances were of enjoying the same pleasures I so enthusiastically sought DOWN HERE. As is my custom when I have far too much time on my hands and no restraints on my thoughts, I began to write. Sorry, it's what I do. The working title of the original manuscript is *THE ETERNAL SCHTUP.* Who knows, between now and the time of publication, it could change. Several times. For those of you who were not blessed with Jewish Russian / Polish grandparents like I was, who spoke Yiddish as their first and usually only language, shtup is a rather crude Yiddish term for sexual intercourse. At times it may be spelled schtup.

A good example would be, "I'd love to *shtup* that hot looking *shikseh* sitting over there." *Shikseh* meaning a most tempting non Jewish female.

My grandparents, bless their souls, would never have used such vulgar language. My *zaideh* (grandfather) may have thought it; but would never have said it out loud. My *bubba,* (grandmother) would have beaten him over the head with her old, oil encrusted iron skillet. And he outweighed her by a good hundred pounds.

It was politely suggested, by everyone, and I do mean everyone, I should change the name of the book. Time for a confession. I have a bad habit. Actually I have many. Far too many to write about here. I rarely if ever, listen to suggestions. They may be right and make me wrong. My frail ego may not take it. Also, I do not use an outline. When finished with one thought, I have no idea what the next thought / chapter will be about. It is called free association; or as many would rightfully say, total lack of good writing skills and a complete lack of discipline.

My second, third and even fourth titles, including **Audacious Conversations with HIM,** where no better.

Oh, one last comment. When I use all caps, like HIM, or HE, I am referring to G-D, or as HE likes to think of himself, Ruler of the Entire Universe.

Bold letters means HE is talking.

Script signifies what HE is thinking.

Who am I to dispute HIS word? Especially when this book is about some really wacky conversations with HIM; about love and life and yes, even about shtupping.

In the truly unimaginable event that HE is actually listening or reading this book, it is one hundred percent a figment of my overactive imagination. Honest to HIM. It's just a joke. Some would suggest, a rather bad joke.

Not me.

Thanks.

Roy Sanders,

Fall / Winter 2017, East Coast, Florida

Prologue

"We've been here almost a week."

Max gave his younger brother Benny a look of total distain.

"It's been only three days and our father is dying. How can you be so damn callous? Can you show just a morsel of respect, forget about all your big deals in New York and just sit here quietly. Maybe pray."

Benny was too busy texting to reply. His fingers were moving at the speed of light. He hated Florida; it was full of old people. It had to be the world capital for canes, walkers, wheel chairs and portable oxygen kits. He hated hospitals or anything that reminded him of death.

He was clearly here under duress.

Max controlled the estate. Benny was never told how big it was or how much he would get. His father had been in the wholesale diamond business all his working life. Benny had heard rumors of the soft suede bag of uncut stones since he was a kid. Part of it belonged to him – as long as he behaved.

Down the hall from the waiting area in Room 117 was Morris Weinstein, formerly from The Bronx, most recently living in Delray Beach, Florida and presently a resident in Hospice of Boca Raton. The building was fairly new, one story and painted in bright colors. Red, yellow and even splashes of orange. It was meant to convey a sense of joy. More like Disney than a chapel or where sick elephants go to die. Regardless of the *let's pretend* décor, a hospice was sadly, still a hospice.

The private room had one bed and two chairs. It could have been a nursery for old people, without the mobiles. There were balloons painted on the ceiling. It was not designed for long term stays. Next to Morris sat Esther, his loving and faithful wife of fifty three years. She had been in the chair for the past three and half hours. Her *tush* was killing her. She was afraid to leave. The bed, G-d forbid, could be empty when she got back. The look of pain on Morris' face, the down turn of his mouth, was killing her. Actually it was killing him. Everyone knew the prostate cancer had spread and it was a matter of days, maybe hours, at the most.

Morris feebly reached the rubber morphine pump and squeezed as hard as his bony hands would allow. He could see the drip, drip, drip; he could feel the pain ease a bit. He tried to relax. He couldn't.

Think of something pleasant Morris, think of something pleasant, he said to himself.

Morris tried. The twinkle in his eyes was long gone. What could be pleasant about dying? He was not ready. He had a great deal of living to do. He would try. What did he have to lose? Nothing. Suddenly a vision came to him. He could not tell if it was real or a drug induced dream. The morphine did crazy things with his mind.

Then a big smile crossed his face and he peacefully closed his eyes.

For the very last time.

The all too human, Morris Weinstein, with all his many faults, was no longer a citizen of Earth.

1

The light was almost blinding.

Everything seemed either stark or subtle shades of white. He was standing on a large cloud or what looked like a cloud. He had only seen them from the window of a plane or far away while on the ground. It was tough to tell their composition. Morris was wearing a short white gown or was it a Roman toga. He wasn't sure. It appeared trimmed in gold. It looked fitted. It also looked new and expensive. He felt no pain. In fact he felt good, very good. He felt like he was thirty five years old, a very good time as he recalled. It was when he was banging the cleaning lady after hours. Her name was Consuelo; she was only twenty two years old and already had two children. Just no husbsand. Morris would slip her an extra fifty every once in a while. It was a good arrangement for both of them. It was then he looked down. His toga was sticking out below the waist. He had an erection. He obviously had been thinking about Consuelo - Again.

Morris Weinstein, age seventy four years old at his death, was now in heaven. There was no question about it.

ROY SANDERS

Why didn't someone tell me about this before? Why did I have to suffer Down There? Why did I have to put up with my nagging wife and unappreciative sons for all these years?

Morris wanted to scream for joy. To rush and tell everyone he was now free. He didn't have to. They already knew. They all smiled at him. No one said a word, they didn't have to. It took Morris a minute or two to realize no one was old or at least looked old. He looked around for a mirror. There were none. There was no reason. You were who you were. Others accepted you, to use a trite phrase, at face value.

Tentatively he stood up. Morris was not sure how to walk on a cloud. It felt soft yet solid. It felt secure. He saw a group of young men, much younger than himself, a few yards off sitting around a table, maybe playing cards and decided to investigate. He was conscious of two separate phenomena. One, he still had an erection and two; there were dozens of beautiful young ladies smiling at him. Morris smiled back; he had not had a woodie for the past few years.

I'm in heaven and so far, no one has told me I'm acting improperly.

The men were playing pinochle. He quietly walked up behind the group to observe. It had been years since he played. Never enough time. By the time he got from Rockefeller Center, the heart of the diamond district in Manhattan to University Avenue in The Bronx, had dinner and listened to the problems of the day from Esther, he was way too tired to play cards. Or make small talk. He would usually fall asleep on the couch with the TV on. He slept through hundreds of reruns of his favorite programs.

"Morris, take a chair and sit down. We've been waiting for you. For years. We were not sure you would make it up here."

His erection had disappeared. He hoped it was only a temporary situation.

"Excuse me, do I know you?"

"Know me, *schmuck*, I saw your ugly face every day for almost thirty five years. I had the shop next to yours on East Forty Ninth Street."

Morris looked more closely.

"Sam? Sammy Glickman? That can't be you. You look like you're thirty five years old. My G-d, you must be ninety by now."

"Please don't use HIS name like that, it offends HIM. If I were still alive, I would be eighty eight."

Morris did some quick arithmetic.

"You never did count very well Sam. Especially at the cash register. You were eighty one when you died and that had to be more than ten years ago. So how does that add up to eighty eight?"

"You're right, but who's counting? And who cares? Sit down and tell us what you have been up to, when you died and how?"

Morris sat down and began to recall when he was first diagnosed with the dreded C word..

He felt like he had been talking nonstop for hours. There was so much to catch up on. Finally he looked around at the group he had not seen for years and years.

The old gang from the Diamond District.

"What time is it? Where can we go for a bite to eat? Maybe deli."

In unison, the group broke up laughing.

"What did I say that was so funny?"

"What time is it? There is no time here. There are no clocks or watches or bell towers. No reason. This is eternity. There are no restaurants here either. We do not have food or drink. All we are all spirits. The body, what you think you see, is an aberration.

"What about all those women I saw. The young, tight body ones, the ones just waiting to be taken. Are you telling me they're not real? Their bodies are not real? Please don't say that."

THE ETERNAL SHTUP

"Sorry Morris. They're all spirits. They are like clouds. And by the way, that woodie you had a few hours ago, that was not real either. It was something you dreamed up and made you feel good. You can get it back anytime you want. Just wish it back. If it makes you feel young and virile.

Morris's chin fell to his chest. None of this was real.

"I think I will lie down for a while. Too much excitement for one day."

It then occurred to Morris; he had no idea where to lie down. Did he have a home or an apartment or just a room? Was it in a nice hotel or a flop house? He was getting nervous. It was all so new and different. Did someone know he was now here and was his name in some type of book or register?

Sam took him by the arm.

Morris was not sure how long he slept. He assumed he had been sleeping. He was also not sure where he was. It felt like a cottage with a room to lie down and a living room to read or entertain. He walked around and was struck by the fact there was no bathroom and no kitchen. That made absolutely no sense. Then he recalled what Sam and the others had told him.

If I do not eat or drink, there is no need for a kitchen or bathroom. If my body is not real, there probably is no need for a bath tub or shower.

ROY SANDERS

When he was alive, a concept he was not comfortable acknowledging yet, he never took a bath. He would rise at six thirty, take a fast shower, get dressed, have coffee and a bagel with Esther and take the A train into Manhattan.

I guess that means no more coffee and garlic bagels.

He also thought about the salt pretzels with mustard he ate on the subway.

Morris was not a gourmet but he liked his food, even the so called meals Esther made for him. She tried; he had to give her that. During the day he would order in; a hot pastrami on rye, some real coleslaw and a Dr. Brown celray. Maybe a black and white large cookie for dessert.

Now, what is there to hold in my hand while I am talking?

Being dead was becoming very strange. Morris had a lot to think about. And all the time in the world to do it. Maybe all of eternity.

2

Shtupping. What about schtupping, he wondered?

Morris was referring to fornicating, having sex, intercourse. Something as much a part of his life as brushing his teeth – or cheating on his wife. He considered himself always a good provider if not exactly a faithful husband.

I guess even cheaters and fornicators can get into heaven. I wonder about lawyers and politicians?

He had very recently experienced a boner. That was real, no figment of his imagination. He saw it, he even briefly touched it. No one saw. The question was, could he use it. His new friends said no. He did not have a real body; all he had was a spirit.

I don't believe it.

He was about to go outside when he realized there was no door to the cottage. How was he to get out? How would he get back in? What about locks and security systems. If they took in cheaters, wouldn't they admit burglars?

I have nothing for anyone to steal. I did not take my household goods when I made the big transition. I have no money here and even if I did, what would I spend it on?

There are no restaurants. I assume there are no super markets or dry cleaners. I don't suppose there are new or used car dealerships here either. That means no gas stations or repair shops.

While contemplating the state of business and the economy, Morris reached his hand towards the wall. It went through. He took a careful step. One leg was inside, one leg outside to cottage.

This is way too weird.

Morris was not sure where he was, where he was going or how to get there. He saw no cars, truck or taxis. Not even Uber. It looked like wherever he was going, he would have to walk.

He was trying to find a street sign so he knew where he lived and how to get back there when a lovely lady, probably about his age appeared. He had not seen her a minute ago. She was smiling.

Everyone here smiles.

THE ETERNAL SHTUP

"Hello, you're new here. My name is Monika. May I show you around?"

Morris noticed she was not wearing a blue dress. Besides, the other Monica was still down there. He wondered if 'Down There' was the appropriate term.

"Thank you."

Monika smiled again. She took his hand as they began to walk. He had no idea where they were going but it was glorious, a most appropriate term, outside. He guessed it was in the mid 70's, no humidity and scattered clouds. Not a hint of rain. Exactly what one would have expected.

"Where are we going?"

"Where would you like to go?"

Morris did not answer immediately. He knew damn well where he would like to go. And do.

"Morris, You are a naughty boy."

Morris blushed.

"If that's what you want, I see no reason why we shouldn't."

Morris realized he was magically back in his cottage, in his bedroom and Monika was standing in front of him. Smiling.

He had no idea how it happened.

"How, um, how did you know?"

"There are no secrets here. We do not hide our feelings. Or desires. There is certainly nothing wrong with wanting to do exotic, what did you call it, shtupping. Am I pronouncing it correctly? I am unfamiliar with the term."

Morris again blushed.

Oh My God, I must really be in heaven.

"Morris, you are. And HE would prefer you not use HIS name like that. If you want to talk to Him, you can use that term. Then it would be perfectly appropriate."

He looked at Monika to see if she was teasing him. She wasn't. He also realized all he was wearing was a robe or tunic. He didn't think he had anything under it and was afraid to look, feel or dwell on it. Monika was also wearing a pure white tunic. It was classic Greek style that crossed her body at the bust. It accentuated her well rounded, well formed chest. He wondered if she was wearing anything under it. He was sure there were no strap lines from a bra but panties? No one walks around heaven without panties.

Or do they?

"Is there any way in particular you would prefer to do it?"

Morris could not believe his ears. He shook his head no. He was not thinking straight. All of a sudden he found he had an erection. The biggest, the best one he ever had. Monika was already on the bed, waiting for him. She was beautiful. She was like a *Playboy* centerfold, only more, well more innocent.

Morris wasted no time.

Surprisingly, he was not exhausted. He was not out of breath. He felt like he was a young stud again. He smiled at Monika.

"Thank you."

"You're welcome but there is no reason to thank me. I too enjoyed it. Or at least I think I did. This was the first time I ever did it like that. You seem to have a great deal of experience. Yes, that's it. You are very experienced."

Morris turned his head away. He was embarrassed. They had been at it for some time and he still had an erection. There was no clock in the room and watches were *verboten*.

If you still have an erection after four hours, consult your doctor.

Morris wondered if there were doctors in heaven. Were their hospitals or ER's or Doc in the Box facilities tucked in the back of pharmacies? Were there even drug stores?

"Shall we go for a walk? There is so much for you to see."

Monika was now standing next to him, her tunic neat and trim and not a hair out of place. She did not ask to use the bathroom to clean up or reapply her makeup.

There's no bathroom. She is not wearing makeup and still looks radiant. We had been at it for who knows how long and ten seconds later she looks like she stepped out from a fashion magazine.

"Of course." he replied.

"Do you play tennis or golf or croquet?

"Maybe a little bit of golf but I was never very good. Never had time to practice or take lessons. Besides, by the time I retired, I was not in such good shape. Not like before, if you get my drift."

"Morris, you are in wonderful shape and you are a terrific lover. I enjoyed everything we did. Would it be alright if we did it again, when you have the time?"

Morris now had a shit-eating grin from one ear to the other. He was not sure he should use the term 'shit eating', it was so vulgar.

I'm going to have to clean up my act. Everyone here knows what I'm thinking.

"Thank you Morris. We appreciate that. You're a very fast learner."

Again the smile and the blush. It was getting to be natural.

3

There were no tee times or wait lists.

There were no Latino workers maintaining the course or riding loud lawn mowers running back and forth to disturb your concentration. The sand traps were all raked and the divots replaced. It looked like the greens had just been resodded and running true. For all practical purposes, Morris could have been at *The Masters,* but it played like a miniature golf course. There was also no swearing or using the Lord's name in vein.

There was no need for it.

Everything was perfect, including the foursome he had been assigned to. There was only one minor distraction. It was Monika. He could not stop thinking about her and it. He was not sure if it was this morning, this afternoon or yesterday. He had no concept of time.

Whenever it was, it was perfect. It was the best I ever had.

ROY SANDERS

"Stop thinking about getting laid so much and concentrate on pitching the ball to within a few feet of the hole. We need to win this hole," said Hogan.

Chi Chi Rodriguez with his funny straw hat, just laughed.

Morris had to let out a big grin. He could not have a single thought that was not broadcast to his three new buddies. He was told he could have sex as often as he wanted, whenever and wherever he wanted, as long as it was not in the middle of a golf match. That would be a sin.

A big sin.

He took out a 52 degree wedge, relaxed his hands and concentrated on sliding the edge of the club under the ball and lifting – and swinging his arms in the follow thru. He let his body go limp to rid him of any tension. Then he swung.

The ball took three small hops before it began to roll. Right into the cup.

"I just made a damn birdie."

He saw the expressions on his partner's face.

"I mean look, I made a birdie. We're one up with three holes to play.

I have to concentrate on what I say or think.

THE ETERNAL SHTUP

Their opponents birdied the last hole. They ended up all even. There were no winners. More importantly, there were no losers. It did not occur to Morris at the time, there were never any losers. They were there to have fun and enjoy each other's company. Morris knew golf was good exercise. Then he remembered, he didn't have to exercise - if he didn't want to.

They walked to the clubhouse, or what Morris assumed was a clubhouse. Their clubs had disappeared after the last hole. There was no place to shower, no need to. As to the bar, there were tables and chairs but nothing to eat or drink. There were no barmaids or cute waitresses to make suggestive remarks to, in the hope one of them would take him up on his constant offers to come down to his shop after work and they could roll in the diamonds.

I've just played a round of golf with Ben Hogan, Chi Chi Rodriguez and someone I've seen on TV years and years ago, but can't think of his last name. Sammie something. It doesn't get any better than this.

"See you guys tomorrow."

Morris was not sure when tomorrow was. Or what time. Or where. He was told not to worry. It would all happen. It has always happened in the past, it would always happen in the future.

What is the future? What does it all mean? Is it really eternity?

Morris was a Jew, not a big surprise to anyone. He was not very religious. Yes, he closed his shop on the first day of Rosh Hashanah and of course on Yom Kippur. The fact was, no one in the Diamond District would have had the *chutzpah* to stay open on the two holiest days of the year. Even if he were open, no self respecting buyer, Jew or not, would enter his little shop of diamonds.

He was Bar Mitzvah, as if he had a choice, like every other thirteen year old in his neighborhood. It was not so much a rite of passage as he was now able to date – to date girls. To spend time alone with them. He was a man, or so he wanted to believe. Besides, there was the whole *megillah* associated with the weekend of tradition. The actual service took place Saturday morning in *shul* with parents, grandparents, relatives from Cleveland and old people he had never met before, from Miami and Boca.

More important were the girls in his high school who he had a crush on or was too afraid to talk to. They would all come. It was an excuse to wear their new outfits. Some of the girls were able to wear strapless dresses.

Those were the ones who now had boobies.

Saturday night was what it was all about. The bartenders knew the kids were only thirteen and fourteen, but they knew the parents of the Bar Mitzvah were the ones who paid them and doling out the tip at the end of the evening.

THE ETERNAL SHTUP

A little wine never hurt anyone. The girls could always claim they were so drunk, two glasses of wine, and did not know the boys were feeling them up. Or at least trying.

As to Morris's belief in G-d, that was a whole different matter. It was not a subject he was comfortable talking about. Certainly not while he was UP HERE.

For the record, there must be a G-d. How else can I explain all this?

It was Morris's standard reply. He had no intention of "explaining all this".

As to whose God was better, Morris wouldn't touch that line with a pole vaulter's stick. It was a loaded question with no right answer.

What is right for you may not be right for me. You believe in who you believe in; I'll believe in who I believe in.

That was his answer and he would be damned if he would ever change it. He never really expected to be where he now was.

Oy vey, I can't think about this anymore. I need to get shtupped again.

"Good afternoon Morris. My name is Rhonda."

I must be dreaming again.

ROY SANDERS

Morris was suddenly transported back in his little cottage. In the sitting room. In front of him stood a twenty five, thirty year old redhead. She was close to five foot ten. She was the most beautiful creature he had ever seen. She was wearing a long white gown. It came to her ankles. She was also wearing gold sandals. Her hair was piled up on the back of her head. The cleavage left little to the imagination.

"Are you well rested from your golf game?"

Morris could not reply. He didn't think he was tired. He didn't care. He could always take some Geritol and a Viagra.

I don't have pills, I don't have a medicine cabinet and if I did, I wouldn't need it anyway.

"I understand you want to make love – again."

Morris looked up at her and nodded his head.

Twice in one day!

4

This is meshugeneh. Totally crazy. Insane.

Morris could not remember the last time he had sex twice in one day with two different women. The fact was; it was never. He was not sure if it were the same day but who cared.

Rhonda was now gone. He was not sure how she got to his cottage, how long she stayed or when she left. All he could recall was the pure white chiffon gown that fell to the ankles and then to the floor. As she stepped out of it, she was naked. Nude. No clothes on. Nothing, not even a bra or a thong. She was beautiful; he had to come up with a new word, a new vocabulary to describe the women. Her skin was almost alabaster. It too was flawless.

This time she was the master, he was the slave, just as he dreamed it would be. She was his teacher, he was the willing student.

"I insist you do it till you get it right. Do you understand me? I want you to listen and learn."

Morris merely nodded. The last thing he wanted was to disappoint the teacher. He wondered if he could earn his Bachelors degree and if so, could he sign up for the Masters program. Someday he could be part of a Masters and Johnson team and educate the world on proper technique.

For now he was satisfied to glow knowing he had been taught by the best. He was not sure if he needed rest but like chicken soup, it could not hurt.

So this is what UP HERE is all about. You think it, you wish it, and you get it. Why didn't I know about this before? This could be The Eternal Shtup.

"THERE IS MORE TO ETERNITY THAN JUST FORNICATING MORRIS."

The voice scared the living crap out of him. Perhaps 'living' and 'crap' were inappropriate terms. The voice was booming, like a cannon or someone talking through a bull horn. It also sounded very official. It was authoritative yet compassionate.

Morris froze. He knew who had been talking to him. It was HIM.

He looked around. There was no one there. He walked into the other room. Still no one or nothing.

"I'm sorry if I offended you. No one told me the rules. I'm not sure what I'm doing. I apologize."

THE ETERNAL SHTUP

"NO NEED TO APOLOGIZE MORRIS. YOU WILL LEARN BY DOING. AS ALL MY CHILDREN DO. NOW IT'S TIME FOR YOU TO REST."

Morris was afraid to look up. He crawled into bed and closed his eyes. He knew HE was watching him.

Maybe shtupping is not so important. Did I just say that? What else is there?

Morris put his head down on the pillow. He was afraid to close his eyes. He was afraid to fall asleep and dream. Most of his dreams were about sex. Morris had no idea how long he slept. It was light out. It was always light out. It was another beautiful day or was it merely a continuation of yesterday. And was there a yesterday or was it all one long, never ending day.

When does it end? When does it become night? How long is eternity?

Morris never thought much about how long eternity was when he was alive. Why would he. Now that appeared to be the only thing on his mind. He refused to think about sex. Well maybe just once in a while but was afraid HE would be listening.

I wonder if masturbating counts?

"YES IT DOES MORRIS."

Morris practically jumped out of his skin. He knew he had to apologize again but was not sure what to say.

Sorry God, I thought jerking off was alright.

"DON'T PISS ME OFF MORRIS. YOU HAVE HEARD OF MY WRATH I ASSUME. BY THE WAY, YOU HAVE NO SKIN TO JUMP OUT OF."

Morris assumed it was just a saying. He didn't really think he could actually be subject to HIS wrath.

Sorry.

"YOU'RE WELCOME."

Morris was not comfortable. Who would be? He wondered if he really was having a conversation with God.

"YES YOU ARE – THINK BEFORE YOU SPEAK AND BE CAREFUL WHAT YOU THINK. OVER AND OUT."

Sorry, again.

Morris sat on the edge of the bed not moving. Trying desperately not to think. He wished he could talk to somebody but who would believe him? Certainly none of the *gonifs* back at the diamond district. His wife, was she now his widow, would accuse him of drinking too much. His two sons would have him committed, but you cannot commit a dead man.

THE ETERNAL SHTUP

"Hi my name is Veronica, do you want to talk. And I mean talk only."

Morris looked up at the olive skinned girl with coal black eyes, long black hair to the small of her back.

"You're beautiful."

The line was becoming over used.

"How did you know?"

Veronica smiled.

What was not to know?

She was wearing all white. How unusual. She had on a simple short white dress that stopped just above the knees. She had on a gold lame belt that made her waist look smaller and everything else much bigger. Morris prayed he would not get an erection. G-d must have been listening. It just laid there on its side not moving an inch.

"Morris, obviously you know HE is all forgiving. UP HERE is a place of love and peace and being happy. There is a big difference between what you call shtupping and what most people think of as making love."

Morris knew exactly what she meant. You make love to one woman, you shtup many.

But this is heaven; I should be able to do whatever I want.

"DON'T PUSH THE ENEVELOPE MORRIS."

Morris and Veronica sat there motionless.

Finally Morris got up the nerve to talk. He knew every word, every thought, was being heard by HIM. He wondered if HE actually recorded all conversations.

"I DON'T HAVE TO MORRIS. I HAVE A VERY GOOD MEMORY. PLEASE DO NOT FORGET WHO I AM."

How can I?

"DON'T BE A SMART ASS MORRIS. I HATE TO SAY IT, BUT YOU'LL BE SORRY."

Sorry.

For the next ten minutes, Morris no longer had a concept of time, the two of them sat on the couch in silence. It could have been ten seconds or ten hours, it really didn't make a difference.

Without a warning Veronica took his hand in both of hers. She held it for a while before talking. Morris was afraid to talk or even think.

"Morris, may we have a personal conversation. I know I have only meet you a short time ago but you seem very honest, know what you want and are not afraid to ask for it. You also seem to have fun bending the rules."

THE ETERNAL SHTUP

Morris had no idea what Veronica had in mind but just looking at the Latino beauty made him shiver.

"I seem to have nothing else to do. What's on your mind?"

Veronica took a deep breath, expanded her lungs to the point the buttons on her dress were about to pop and just blurted it out.

"Will you be my boyfriend? Can I be your girlfriend? Then whenever we want, we can make love, just not how you say it, shtupping."

Morris was afraid to say anything. He was afraid to think anything. He knew you-know-who was listening.

Till death do us part. That's what my wedding vows said. Marriage, on earth, had finality to it. Once I died, I was no longer married to Esther and logically she was free to do what she wanted to do.

That was the reasoning of Morris as he contemplated his new found status. It was not the greatest of marriages but they had kept that piece of gossip to themselves. Morris wondered how he would fill out a dating application. He did not know he or anyone needed Match.com or Christian Mingles.com.

Hmm, Single, Married, Divorced, Dead. The last one seems to fit the bill.

"Do you think you could learn to love me?"

'I just know I could, when can we start?" Veronica teasingly replied.

"How about right now? I think we are now going steady. Is that alright?"

"Of course. Now will you please take off my belt and dress, it is way too confining for our new relationship."

My kind of girl.

"SMART MOVE MORRIS. VERY SMART MOVE."

Morris had a big grin on his face. He now had the blessing of the one person that really mattered.

HIM.

"Oh G-d. Thank you."

"YOU'RE WELCOME MORRIS."

5

"Congratulations Morris."

"Best of luck, kid."

"How did you do it, you sly fox?"

News spread like wildfire. More like the word of G-d. It seemed like everyone who saw Morris, and they were all over heaven, heard about Veronica and him. After all, they had HIS blessings. It was not as if Morris was trying to circumvent the wishes of the Almighty or find a way to have sex indiscriminately. They were officially 'almost engaged'.

Morris did not know where Veronica actually lived. He assumed she had a cottage just like his. He knew she was from Bogota, Colombia, not that it really mattered. She never mentioned a husband, an ex husband or any children. He felt if she wanted to talk about it, he would gladly listen but up here, the past was the past.

The days seemed to blend into one another. He was never sure if it was today, still yesterday or already tomorrow, not that it really mattered.

He played golf every day. Again, he assumed it was every day. After his match, again a tie, Veronica asked him to join her in a lecture series that was given by five of the all time great philosophers.

"Please, please, please. Everybody will be there. I would just die if we missed it."

Veronica realized her bad choice of words.

"Tell me again, who will be on the panel?"

"Well there is St. Thomas Aquinas, who claimed he proved the existence of God. He is always a big favorite. Master Kong Qiu, we all call him by his Christian name Confucius, who tells everyone who will listen that he came up with the principals of ethics and politics, Rene Descartes, the real father of modern philosophers and the two old timers who argue with everyone and everything at these seminars; Plato and Aristotle. They have been at it forever or what seems like forever."

Morris had planned on watching a celebrity golf match at the same time between Bobby Jones and Arnie. He knew they played the North course at least once a week. He realized he would have to get the new AppleSoft 15 that kept track of everything by just thinking of what he wanted to remember. And automatically reminded him of it.

THE ETERNAL SHTUP

"Alright I'll go, but you owe me."

"When do you want to collect Big Boy?"

The next thing he knew, they were both back in his cottage. In the bedroom.

I know I'll get tired of this someday. Just not today.

"Your choice of which way."

"Thanks, you're so good to me."

The big surprise at the lecture was the moderator. It was HIM.

Tommy Aquinas was thrilled. It was he who first postulated the very existence of HIM. Now HE was the panel moderator. Confucius was not pleased at all but said nothing. He didn't have to. Everyone, including HIM, knew what he was thinking.

Again, that demanding, authoritative and booming voice.

Did he not ever speak like a normal person?

Apparently not.

"DO I DISPLEASE YOU BY BEING HERE TODAY, CONFUCIUS?"

"You might have given me some notice so I could have properly prepared my notes better."

"AS I RECALL, AND WE ALL KNOW WHAT A GOOD MEMORY AND HOW ACCURATE I AM, YOU DIED IN 479 BC. THAT'S MORE THAN 2,500 YEARS AGO. SURELY THAT SHOULD HAVE GIVEN YOU ENOUGH TIME TO PREPARE. WOULD YOU BE SO KIND AS TO INTRODUCE YOUR ESTEEMED COLLEAGUES AND MAKE THE APPROPRIATE OPENING REMARKS?"

It was not a question or a request. It was his typical, all embracing power play.

Confucius nodded.

Morris could not believe what he was seeing and hearing. It was better than reality TV.

The cloud was very comfortable as he laid his head in Veronica's lap. By the time Rene Descartes prepared to make his case, Morris was fast asleep. At the first sign of snoring, Veronica gave him a slight nudge. He did not stop. She gave him a slightly more vigorous nudge and whispered in his ear,

"Come on."

"Now."

"No. Not now. You were disturbing others with your loud breathing. Don't you ever think of anything else?"

"Not when you're around. I even think of it when you're not around. You know, you are the best. And I should know."

"Braggart. Go back to sleep."

THE ETERNAL SHTUP

Morris moved the side of his head from her lap up to her ample bosom.

He was now thinking how he could get another 20, 30 yards out of his new driver. Maybe he would ask Gene Sarazen the next time he saw him at the practice range. He had been up here for the past fifteen or so years. Gene played every day. Morris assumed it was every day.

Veronica could not get enough of Plato and Aristotle. She had read everything she could, in Spanish, about the two of them when she was in *universidad*.

When the lecture / debate was over, everyone simply disappeared. There was no mad rush for the exit rows. There were no exit rows – or exit signs. There was no stampede to the parking lots. There were no cars so no need for parking lots.

Everyone simply went on to what was next.

Veronica and Morris were magically transported back in his cottage. It was now home. He wondered where her home had been and what personal items she had left in it. The only thing he could think of was clothes. Clothes consisted of simple, well tailored dresses, gowns or togas and sandals. To his knowledge, Veronica owned or wore no intimate apparel. This included underwear and nightwear. She had no need for coats or jackets or gloves or mittens or hats or scarves. He wondered how her hair was always so beautiful, like she brushed it one hundred times every morning. He wondered if she shampooed and conditioned it. There were no wash basins or showers. He wondered what happened to all the hair dressers and beauty parlors and tanning salons.

Morris wondered about a lot of things.

I have not had a hair cut since I died. It was gray, what I had left of it, then. Now it's thick, brown and wavy. And I don't need a trim. Or a shave. It's a miracle.

Everything in heaven was a miracle.

"Would you take my robe off me, please?"

Morris was never one to complain about a task or shun a request from a charming young lady. One apparently in constant need of satisfaction. Complete and total satisfaction.

"Of course my dear."

When they awoke it was morning. It had to be morning. They had been at it for hours and hours and fell asleep in each other's arms. They were exhausted or at least should have been. It had been the warm blooded Columbian who was the aggressor. Enough was not enough. More meant more and more and more. If he were the age he was when he died, he would have died all over again.

Morris looked down at his body. It was trim and fit. The stomach was flat and ripped. He tried to remember when the last time he looked like that — if ever? It had to have been in his mid to late twenties when he had received a medical discharge from the Marine Corp and vowed he would never grow old and fat and lazy.

The incident was still the only thing he ever regretted. He recalled it like it was yesterday.

It was a typical thirty three mile hike with full field pack. They were in Paris Island, the home of Marine Corp basic training. It was hot, muggy and the thirty seven pound pack was cutting into my shoulders. I was not the only one suffering, and I knew it. During a ten minute break the D I decided he needed to set an example of discipline. Yea, he chose me. "Give me twenty, dirt bag." I looked at my drill instructor. I was hurtin, big time and twenty pushups with full field pack was just about more than I wanted to handle.

"Sarge, give me a break. Quit busting my balls. We just did thirty some miles in under four hours. That has to be some type of freakin platoon record." The drill sergeant went crazy calling me every name in the book. I cracked and told him the only thing he was good for was making life miserable for normal, sane people. The other Leather Necks could not believe I had the nerve, the balls, the shear audacity, to talk back to a D.I. I guess I was about to be put in chains or whipped with a cat-of-nine tails or whatever they do to assholes like me, when I collapsed. Maybe the smartest thing I ever did.

I woke up the next day in the hospital. Turns out I had an embolism floating around in my brain. It could have killed me. Rather than six months in the stockade and then a dishonorable discharge, they got rid of me the quick and easy way; a medical, unfit for combat, discharge.

When the drill sergeant heard about it, he went ape shit.

Morris vowed he would look and act and stay in shape after his discharge. In his mind he was still a Marine. He didn't have time or money to join a fancy gym so he spent fifty-five dollars, what seemed like a fortune at the time, to buy a complete set of weights. They were kept in the basement, what he fondly called *Morris' Mighty Gym*. He had a used gym mat and an old wooden table that he cut the legs off at about ten inches. This was his workout bench.

Twice a day, before work at around six thirty in the morning and when he got home, before dinner, he would sneak downstairs and pump iron for twenty, twenty five minutes. The Marines had taught him discipline.

That was forty years ago. Look at me now. I am no more than twenty eight, twenty nine years old and have spent all last night shtupping a hot Latin lover.

How the hell did I do it?

Morris immediately regretted the use of the terms *shtupping* and 'how the hell'. He was waiting for the booming voice to remind him of his mistake. Instead he saw a vision or what he assumed was a vision. It was a large forefinger in front of him waving back and forth. He did not have to ask whose finger it was or what the message was.

THE ETERNAL SHTUP

He clearly understood. He silently mouthed the word, "Sorry".

The finger disappeared.

I'll just have to be more careful. Don't want to pi, don't want to do anything to make him upset. This is too good a gig to blow.

6

Morry, for some unknown reason he now thought of himself as Morry, a name he acquired in high school, thought about his new roommate, new partner, new almost fiancée. Veronica was still sound asleep, her long brown hair spread over her chest. She reminded him of long suppressed memories. Memories of Layla.

My G-d, that was more than forty years ago. She was a doctor and lived in Bogotá. She desperately wanted to move to the USA. There was a brain drain restriction in Colombia at the time. The state did not want to lose their doctors, scientists or PhD's. There were no restrictions on lawyers. They could all leave as far as the government was concerned.

Morry was at a diamond convention in Colombia when he had a touch of indigestion. He knew it had to be the food. By ten that evening the pain became so severe and he was sure he was having a coronary. He called the front desk and within a half hour he was looking up at the largest brown eyes he had ever seen.

THE ETERNAL SHTUP

"Who are you and why are you unbuttoning my shirt?"

"My name is Dr. Guzman, I am a cardiologist. The hotel stated you were in severe stress. I am about to listen to your heart."

"You're the Doc?"

"I am. Now just lay there, try to relax and breathe normally."

Morry's eye darted from her eyes, to her substantial cleavage to the stethoscope she was listening through. If he ever wanted a heart attack, this was it. Just the thought of mouth to mouth made his pulse jump a good twenty points.

"Please sit up."

"The doc listened placed the stethoscope on several parts of his back and asked him to breathe heavily. No *problemo,* he thought.

The next afternoon Dr. Guzman called, merely as a courtesy. Morry asked if he could ask her a few professional questions as to his heart, perhaps over a drink at the hotel bar.

Dr. Layla Zerya Guzman agreed.

It developed into far more than an affair. It lasted three years and close to thirty round trips from JFK to BOG, El Dorado International Airport in the northwest section of Bogota.

Morry did not worry about luggage. All he needed was a small carryon for toiletries. His actual clothes were safely kept at her small two bedroom condo.

Layla and Veronica could have been sisters. Why they could have almost been twins.

Morris reached down and gave Veronica – or was it Layla – a quiet, tender kiss on the forehead.

Veronica opened her eyes, smiled sleepily and thanked him. He was not sure for what.

He was about to ask her if she would like a cup of coffee. He wanted to make some breakfast; fried eggs, hash browns, rye toast loaded with salt butter and perhaps a tall glass of O J.

I wonder why there is no food here. It's a great way to kill the morning and discuss what we want to do today.

THERE IS NO REASON FOR FOOD OR DRINK HERE. WE DO NOT 'KILL' THE MORNING HERE. THERE IS EVERY ACTIVITY YOU CAN POSSIBLY IMAGINE HERE. WHY DON'T YOU TAKE SOME ART CLASSES FROM LEONARDO TODAY?

Morris bit his tongue. He hated to be told what to do and when to do it. Now he could not even think it.

Perhaps heaven is not all it's cracked up to be?

Morris prayed no one heard that thought. It was blasphemy.

"Let's take a walk to the Arts and Craft center. Da Vinci is giving a class there today," Veronica suggested.

They did not actually walk there. They had no idea where it was and there were no gas stations or book stores to pick up a street map. Morris briefly wondered if there was a local Chamber of Commerce. They would have maps of everything.

NO THERE'S NOT MORRIS. BESIDES, YOU ARE HERE ALREADY.

Morris and Veronica were now standing in front of a replica of the Sistine Chapel. He wondered if it was really a . . .

YES IT IS.

Siri would definitely be out of a job here.

DO YOU KNOW WHY WE DO NOT SEND DONKEYS TO COLLEGE?

Before Morris could think of an answer, the reply came back, loud and clear.

"NO ONE LIKES A WISE ASS MORRIS. FORGET SIRI. AND SAY HELLO TO LENNY FOR ME. BY THE WAY, I DON'T LIKE THE NAME MORRY".

So now he's a comedian.

"WHAT'S THE MATTER MORRIS. DON'T YOU LIKE COMEDIANS?"

Morris refused to even think of an answer.

"MAYBE YOU'D LIKE TO MEET ONE OR TWO. SAY BOB HOPE OR ABBOTT AND COSTELLO. OR ONE OF YOUR KIND, SAY BUDDY HACKETT. SORRY, LENNIE BRUCE DID NOT MAKE IT HERE. I FELT SORRY ABOUT THAT, BUT RULES ARE RULES. HE JUST WOULDN'T FIT IN."

HE was thinking. Bruce wrote his own material. Something Hope never did.

Again, Morris did not answer.

At the entrance of the building stood the individual called the most diversely talented man who had ever lived.

"Good day Mr. Da Vinci, HE asked me to say hello to you."

Da Vinci merely nodded.

Big deal, so HE's watching what I am doing today.

The man looked lost. His blonde beard and hair were tangled in one, all the way past his neck. He was wearing a funny style black hat, almost like the Greek sailors, but slightly different. It was probably his own design. If he didn't like something or wanted something new, he designed or invented it. It was his eyes that bothered everyone. He was studying everyone and everything at the same time. He refused to look you in the eyes if and when you had a conversation with him. You got the impression he was telling you, "I'll speak with you only if I think you have something important to say – and frankly I don't."

Morris was quick to notice how Leonardo was staring at Veronica. It was as if he were visually undressing her, not that it would have taken more than ten seconds. Da Vinci had positioned himself so anyone in front of him had the sun directly behind them. Veronica was wearing a simple white cotton dress. She had on no underwear and the sun was shining through the light weight garment. For all practical purposes, she was standing in front of Mr. Inventor *Extraordinaire* completely naked. He made no bones about it; he was focused on her exceptionally large nipples.

Morris immediately stepped between the two of them.

"Why don't you go off and invent the x ray machine. That way you won't have to stand in the hot sun all day to get your rocks off."

Lennie knew the X ray machine was discovered, by accident by German physicist Wilheim Rontgen in 1895, some three hundred seventy six years after he died.

Veronica realized what Da Vinci was doing and turned her back to him. She was heard to mumble to all those within ten feet, "Dirty old man."

"HA."

There were no secrets in heaven, not even for one of the greatest painters, sculptures' inventors of all time.

HE was having himself a good laugh.

Lennie tried to take one last look at Veronica, scowled and left.

I have seen better in my day. I think The Chapel could use a touch up.

"Well now that we blew him off, what do you want to do today?"

Veronica coyly smiled, "What would you like to do?"

Morris just shook his head. She was truly amazing.

Morris had a habit of looking at women's jewelry, usually diamonds. It was an occupational habit. In this case the rock in question was nestled in the cleavage of the head golf pro that was obviously just waiting to give another lesson to whoever wanted one. It had to be a brilliant three and a half carat round hung from a twenty inch platinum chain. Rather than being tight just below the neck, high up on the torso, it rode low between her magnificent breasts. As she swung the club, the perfect stone moved from one breast to another.

Morris was fascinated.

"Do you usually stare so intently?"

THE ETERNAL SHTUP

Morris blushed, "I was looking at your chest."

"Yes, I know. I could feel your eyes penetrating me."

"No, I mean I was looking at the diamond solitaire just resting, um, I'm a diamond merchant, I mean I was and the stone looks absolutely perfect. Do you mind if I take a closer look?"

"I don't seem to be able to stop you, do I?"

Morris did not hear her last remark. He had his head not three inches from the stone.

"Beautiful, absolutely beautiful."

"Why thank you. They are nice, aren't they? My name's Tiffany. Are you finished looking. I do have a face and a full complement of other well preserved body parts you know."

"Excuse me."

Morris was not sure what she was talking about but it seemed like she was flirting with him or at least putting him on.

She was wearing a white, short pleated golf skirt and white collared polo shirt. An outfit like that and the motion of swinging a golf club absolutely demanded appropriate under garments.

Morris could see no OPL or the hint of a bra where the diamond rested. The skirt apparently was lined to hide the obvious panty line.

"Do I meet with your approval?"

"I was just thinking of something else. Sorry."

"WE ALL KNOW WHAT YOU ARE THINKING ABOUT MORRIS. YOU SEEM TO HAVE A ONE TRACK MIND. BY THE WAY, WHERE'S VERONICA?"

Morris was about to tell HIM to mind his own business when he realized, everything was obviously HIS business.

Tiffany pretended she had not heard the reprimand.

"Would you like to practice your swing or perhaps your grip? You would be surprised how far you can drive the ball with a more relaxed but firm grip on the shaft."

Morris was trying hard, poor term, was trying desperately, not to think about Veronica or the thought of the grip on his shaft.

"Come here, and relax. Let me do the work."

With that Tiffany stood directly behind him, actually pushing into him, put her arms around him and paced his hands overlapping, on the driver now in his hand.

"Don't grip it so tightly. Just swing your arms back and forth like this."

She squeezed him tightly and began to swing their arms in unison from side to side.

Her breasts were drilling two deep holes in his back. He felt his arms relax and his dick grow hard. He had to get the hell out of there. Soon.

"I'm sorry; I have to be somewhere else. I'll be back later."

Much later, like twenty years, Morris thought.

"SMART MOVE MORRIS. YOU'VE GOT MORE ON YOUR PLATE THAN YOU CAN ALREADY HANDLE."

HE's right. I do.

Morris was now back at his own cottage. Veronica was sitting on the couch, waiting.

He did not know what to say. He didn't have to.

"Did you enjoy your mini golf lesson? You didn't have to stop on my account you know. There is no such thing as jealousy UP HERE. Besides, Tiffany is a very good instructor. In all sort of swings. She seems to be giving lessons all day long. Every day."

Morris was sure she was telling him something but was afraid to ask for clarification. He did not want to ruin a good thing. A damn good thing.

HE said I had more on my plate than I can already handle.

"YES I DID MORRIS."

This time the voice was a mere whisper. Still, there was no question who said it.

Morris was totally confused. It seemed Veronica was saying yes, go for it, I don't mind and HE was telling him it was not a good idea. HE certainly held all the aces. It was HIS house, HIS game and HIS cards.

He didn't need any more golf lessons and his grip had not been this relaxed since his days in Bogota. He briefly though of Layla. Then he looked at Veronica, her double.

"It's alright to think of her, it does not bother me. We all have had past lovers. Many past lovers. It is natural you should think of her. It is a compliment to me. She was very beautiful. And no we were never related."

"Thank you, you are the best."

"No Morris, I am good, very good as you already know, but I am not the best. You have only been here a very short time. You will see."

Morris said nothing. He decided he needed a nap. A long nap.

Alone.

7

Morris found himself back at the driving range. He was not sure if it was the next day or the day after that. It made no difference.

"Hello Morris. I know Veronica had a little talk with you. There is no competition here. We are all here for the same reason. To relax, to enjoy, to have fun."

Morris blushed. He looked up at Tiffany. She was wearing the same outfit. It looked a little tighter around the bust.

"Are you ready for your first lesson?"

Morris nodded.

Tiffany moved behind him and put her hands over his. He could feel the pressure up and down his spine. He was trying to relax but it was not happening.

"Close your eyes Morris and pretend your body is jelly."

Morris closed his eyes.

"Now open them."

He did.

They were no longer on the golf course or the practice tee. They were in a small cottage. In the bedroom. He could not tell if it was his bedroom or not.

"You're dying to know if I have anything on under my skirt and polo shirt. Now would probably be a good time to find out."

Morris was a bundle of nerves. He was not sure who he was afraid of most. HE was at the top of the list. Veronica was a distant second.

"Morris, you are going to have to learn to relax your hands. Think of my body as a trigger on the rifle you carried while in the Marines. Do not jerk. Squeeze, just gently squeeze. I promise you, nothing will break. And Morris, HE understands."

Morris felt like he was back in high school, trying to unhook Mary Ann's bra while pretending to watch the movie. He was all thumbs. After three unsuccessful tries, Mary Ann reached behind and undid it herself. They fell out of their cotton prison like two overripe tomatoes.

Tiffany raised her arms so Morris could lift her golf shirt up over her head. There was no reason to unhook any bra. There was none. For a grown man who had had sex with more women than he could count, he began to sweat. He was back in the car, in the drive-in, with Mary Ann. You never forget the name of your first. Or second. Sometimes your third.

"I'm waiting."

Morris stared at Tiffany. She did not have an ounce of fat around her belly. She was waiting for him to remove her shorts. She looked to the zipper on the side. Morris pulled it down in one quick motion and stepped back. No panties. More important, a tight ass and tight thighs and Lord knows. *I swear I did not mean it that way*, what else. He was quickly becoming a mass of sweat.

RELAX MORRIS, I UNDERSTAND. ENJOY. THIS ONE'S ON THE HOUSE.

With a firm blessing from HIM and a teacher who could not wait to teach, Morris knew this had to be his lucky day.

"Morris, I am not porcelain or glass, I will not break. I am here for one reason and one reason only. To give you pleasure. Making you happy is reward enough for me. I'm waiting Big Boy."

All semblance of time was lost. It could have been a few hours; it could have been a few days, if that was possible. Just when he thought he could go no more, do no more, a new sense of energy came over him. He felt like the energizer bunny. He kept going and going and going. It was the most amazing, unbelievable, sensual, exhausting, dynamic experience he had ever had.

Thank you God.

It was more of a figure of speech than anything else.

"YOU'RE WELCOME."

Morris clearly did not expect that.

He turned over again to thank Tiffany. She was gone. The golf skirt and top were also gone. The sheets were not even wrinkled or wet. Morris wondered if it had all been a dream. The best dream he had ever had.

"IT WAS REAL MORRIS; YOU CAN TRUST ME ON THAT ONE."

Morris thought, *'If I can't trust God, who can I trust?'*

"NO ONE MORRIS, ABSOLUTELY NO ONE."

Morris rolled over, he definitely needed a nap.

God is on my side, he thought.

"YES I AM."

He always gets the last word.

"YES I DO."

THE ETERNAL SHTUP

"You look wonderful. I assume Tiffany pleased you."

Morris did not know what to say. He did not want to lie and there was no way he could tell Veronica the truth. He shrugged his shoulders as if it say, *It was alright I guess.* Sort of like he had his son wash the car and someone asked if he did a good job.

"Morris, look at me."

What did I do wrong now?

"It's alright that you made love to Tiffany. That is her purpose here; well it is one of her purposes. You should not feel guilty or ashamed. It is not as if you were cheating on me and I did not know exactly what you were doing. Everyone knows. Even HE knows. HE knows everything. If you want to talk about it, that's alright. If Tiff did something special that you liked, let me know so I can please you the same way."

Morris's eyebrows lifted to near his forehead.

Morris wondered if Veronica was also 'fooling around'. Without a sense of time, he had no idea where she was or who she was with when she was not with him.

Am I getting jealous?

"Well, there was one thing,"

"Oh goodie. Tell me exactly what she did. Can we practice now?"

The question required no response.

Morris wondered, *Will this go on forever?*

"THAT'S UP TO YOU MORRIS."

"I stopped by the driving range this morning. To see Tiffany."

Morris looked at Veronica and turned white.

"Whatever for?"

"To thank her, of course. It was the polite thing to do. She is so creative. I would never have thought of it myself. She mentioned if you would like a golf lesson, a real golf lesson, she would be more than happy to squeeze you in later today."

Morris made no response.

"Do you like her better than me?"

"No, of course not. I'm not sure why I even agreed to it."

"I was only teasing you. You know you can have any girl you want here. There is no limit, no quota. This is the place for eternal bliss."

The first thought to come to his mind was, *The Eternal Shtup.*

"Veronica, I think I love you."

THE ETERNAL SHTUP

"Don't be silly. You desire me. You enjoy making love to me. You get off on what I do to you. You want me to do more and more and more. But love, don't even think that way. Just enjoy what you have and know there will always be more. More of everything, including some truly sensual, sexual women. Now let's just forget about those other women for a minute and let me practice what I just learned from Tiffany."

Veronica had a naughty look on her face as she whispered into his ear,

"Come on, let's fuck."

And fuck they did.

8

Morris was walking aimlessly with absolutely nothing on his mind. He noticed an elderly man with a flowing white beard walking by himself. Everyone seemed to give him his space. The man was wearing a long white lab coat and had a stethoscope draped casually around his neck. He walked with a certain air; one of extreme confidence. Almost arrogant.

Morris briefly wondered why he had not seen any hospitals or walk-in clinic or ambulances. Or ambulance chasers. He asked the closest person near him if that was a doctor.

The stranger replied,

"No, no. That's God. He just thinks he is a doctor."

HE overheard and gave the stranger a stern look.

"THEN DON'T COME TO ME WHEN YOU GET SICK"

The stranger lowered his head and walked in the opposite direction.

THE ETERNAL SHTUP

Morris thought, *This is my big chance.*

He carefully approached the bearded ONE.

"Excuse me, may I have a word with YOU."

HE was so impressed with the tenacity of Morris, stopped and sat back on a waiting cloud.

"WHAT CAN I DO FOR YOU MORRIS"

Morris was impressed He knew his name.

"I KNOW EVERYONE'S NAME. YOU FORGET WHO I AM."

"No Sir. I did not forget who you were, uh, are. It's just that there are so many people up here. It must be difficult remembering everyone. I am sorry if I am bothering you."

"DO YOU HAVE A QUESTION MORRIS OR DO YOU JUST WANT TO SHOOT THE BREEZE."

"I'm not sure. I have never spoken to you before, you know, *mano y mano*. I guess I just want to thank you – for everything. This is some place you got here. Sure beats Disney World. Course they have more rides. Guess I am rambling. It was sure good to meet you in person Sir."

"HAVE A NICE DAY MORRIS. PERHAPS YOU CAN KEEP IT IN YOUR PANTS ALL DAY TODAY. IT'S NOT A CONTEST. THERE IS NO GUINNESS BOOK OF RECORDS. THE LADIES WILL ALL BE HERE FOREVER"

HE smiled. He had just made a little joke. Morris did not think it was funny.

He could not wait to tell someone, anyone.

I just spoke to HIM.

"YES YOU DID MORRIS. SO DO MOST PEOPLE. ONLY THIS TIME I ANSWERED YOU. I AM FRIENDLIER THAN MOST PEOPLE THINK."

HE smiled – again. HE made a mental note to himself about Morris. HE wanted to learn more about Morris, maybe make him his new best buddy. Sort of a BFF.

It had been years, decades, centuries, since HE had a best friend forever. The last one was St. Thomas of Aquinas, but they seemed to argue over everything and Tommie was always a sore loser. The friendship lasted less than one hundred fifty years. Clearly not forever.

Morris had no idea what HE was thinking. How could he? He decided today would be a good day to do nothing. Just hang out by himself. He didn't feel like playing golf or the usual.

Maybe I'll do some reading. Haven't done that in years.

The next thing he knew, Morris was at HIS Library. He had no idea how he got there or if this type of transportation would work in Manhattan, the land of eternal gridlock. Definitely better than all those Yellow Cabs.

THE ETERNAL SHTUP

DON'T EVEN THINK ABOUT IT MORRIS. REMEMBER, THERE ARE ONLY SO MANY MIRACLES I HAVE AVAILABLE. WHY WASTE ONE ON THOSE CRAZY NEW YORKERS.

"Ah SIR, I don't mean to be impertinent, but can I ask for a favor?"

"WHAT IS IT THIS TIME MORRIS. I HAVE GIVEN YOU EVERYTHING YOU HAVE ASKED FOR, HAVEN'T I ?"

"Why yes YOU have. I know this may not sound polite, but could you lower your voice an octave or two. It is so booming. It hurts my ears and at times, scares the hell out of me. Sorry about that slip, but you know what I mean, after all, you know everything."

There was a moment of silence. HE was thinking.

"IS THIS BETTER MORRIS?"

"Much. Thanks."

HE thought, *The kids got spunk. I've got to give him that."*

"MIND IF I JOIN YOU IN THE LIBRARY?"

Morris was floored by the request but did not miss a beat in his reply.

"It's your library. Why not? Maybe you could introduce me to a few of your friends. I think I would like that."

Morris was thinking, this will make me some kind of Big Shot up here. Hanging out with HIM.

"I HEARD THAT MORRIS. I JUST THOUGHT IT WOULD BE GOOD IF WE GOT TO KNOW EACH OTHER BETTER."

"Sorry."

"NO NEED TO APOLOGIZE. JUST THINK BEFORE YOU THINK."

"Yes sir."

"YOU DON'T HAVE TO ALWAYS CALL ME SIR. JUST IN FRONT OF THE OTHERS. IF WE ARE GOING TO BE BUDDIES, I WOULD PREFER, IN PRIVATE, THAT YOU CALL ME ABE. YES I THINK I WOULD LIKE THE NAME ABE."

"Ah, alright, Abe."

'COME ON IN. I WANT YOU TO MEET PAPA AND SOME OF HIS OLD CRONIES"

"Do you mean Mr. Hemingway, Abe?

"WHY YES. AND YOU CAN CALL HIM PAPA, NOW THAT HE KNOWS WE ARE BUDDIES."

"Thanks, Abe."

Morris was still having trouble calling HIM, Abe. He was trying to think, without actually thinking. It was giving him

THE ETERNAL SHTUP

a headache. Then he remembered, no one has headaches UP HERE.

The headache suddenly disappeared.

"Papa" Hemingway was clearly the boss, like a giant bull in a china shop. He treated Frank Baum, who he claimed wrote ChildPlay books as some sort of flash in the pan. There was no Oz. As to Jules Verne, there was no question he was doing grass when he wrote *Journey to the Center of the Earth*. How else could he come up with such cockamamie ideas?

HE said nothing but knew Papa and F. Scott Fitzgerald kept a few flasks of bootleg booze hidden for when the two of them were alone. HE, being the forgiving soul HE was, merely turned a blind eye.

Morris was fascinated.

I never knew. I never knew.

All the writers were thinking the same thing. Who is the Morris person and why has HE taken such a liking to him?

HE heard it all.

"BECAUSE HE MAY HAVE FOUND THE SECRET TO ETERNAL HAPPINESS – SHTUPPING."

HE had decided to go back to his original booming voice. It was what they were used to. It clearly made the desired impression. It was still HIS show.

Papa rolled on the floor in laughter. Tears were now streaming down his fat cheeks and onto his trim beard. It was the funniest thing he had heard HIM say in at least fifty years.

Frank Baum had never heard the term and quickly asked Siri though he was not sure of the correct spelling or pronunciation. He was aghast when Siri loudly explained it to him. It was definitely not in good taste he thought.

"GET OVER IT FRANK. LOOSEN UP A LITTLE. IT WON'T HURT TO SMILE NOW AND THEN."

Baum said nothing. What was there to say?

Fitzgerald being a true WASP, turned to Ernie for an explanation. There was now a wink and a nod. He obviously agreed but would never acknowledge it in public.

Morris's face turned bright red. He had no idea what to say or do. So he stood there sheepishly looking at the intricate mosaic floor design.

Probably done by Lennie.

God grinned.

"GOTTCHA."

Everyone laughed, whether they got it or not.

9

"HE approves. He definitely approves. HE told that to Hemingway and Fitzgerald and Baum and Jules Verne and all the gang."

"Whatever are you talking about?"

He was now with Veronica and Tiffany. They were back at his place. They had an arrangement. It was suggested by Veronica. She knew how much Morris enjoyed being with Tiff and the fact Tiffany had an adventurous spirit. Wild may have been a better term. Veronica would do anything to make Morris happy so she found herself at the driving range making a suggestion.

It was to be a surprise to Morris.

Tiffany ate it up like a baby with a dish of strained apple sauce.

Morris had just told the girls that he had spent time with HIM and HE told some very important and influential people that he, meaning Morris **"MAY HAVE FOUND THE SECRET TO ETERNAL HAPPINESS – SHTUPPING."**

"HE actually said that?"

"Swear to G-d, I mean, yes HE did. I have half dozen witnesses. Besides, I would never lie about what HE said."

Tiffany reasoned, "If shtupping one lady is the secret to eternal happiness, just imagine what kind of joy you will receive by shtupping both of us - at the same time.

Morris's ultimate fantasy was about to come true. He was about to thank HIM, but decided to do it in person. Later.

"Where do we start?"

"Use your imagination Lover Boy."

HE never thought of himself as a voyeur but this was too good to pass up. It was not as if he had not seen it all before. He had a quick flash of Sodom and Gomorrah. Now that was a triple X experience. Too bad they did not have cell phones with cameras back then. The internet would have crashed by the volume of traffic.

After a few minutes HE was becoming bored. Same old, same old. There had to be new ways of having sex. HE would think about it later. For now he had a meeting with the Jews and the Arabs. HE had no idea how he could resolve that situation.

THE ETERNAL SHTUP

MAYBE IF I DRAIN ALL THE OIL FROM THE MIDDLE EAST. THEN LET'S SEE WHO REALLY WANTS TO LIVE IN THE DAMN DESERT.

Morris was too busy draining his own oil to worry about anything except pleasing the two nymphs. At times he was not sure who he was pleasing and who was pleasing him. It was one big orgy. This indeed was heaven.

Hours or days later, they all rested. Even HE rested after six days. Morris knew it was not six straight days. That would have been impossible – it just felt like it.

It seemed like everyone was thanking everyone. For Morris and Veronica it had been a first. For Tiff, it was just another great time, one to add to her ever growing resume. For HIM, a welcome diversion from the problems of the day.

HE was now back to thinking, was there another way. None that he could think of. Then The Almighty had a flash, he would ask Tiffany. If anyone had a new way, it surely would be her. HE had seen her at her best.

More than once.

"I don't think we need Tiffany anymore."

Veronica was thrilled but tried not to show it.

"Whatever you say Big Boy."

"I think we both got the hang of what goes where and why."

"And then some," Veronica replied.

She was thinking at this point, a little rest would help.

While she slept, HE was now getting to understand Morris. HE obviously knew what made him tick. HE needed more information.

"MAY WE TALK? CONFIDENTAL"

Tiffany was not sure what to say. Yes was definitely the right answer. The only question was about what. She was not sure what they had in common.

"YOU APPEAR TO HAVE A CERTAIN DEGREE OF EXPERTISE IN YOUR LINE OF, IN WHAT YOU DO BEST."

No further explanation of her expertise was necessary.

"Why thank you."

It had not been rendered as a compliment, merely a statement of fact. Now HE was about to explain his request and found himself embarrassed, a most unusual situation.

"FOR AS LONG AS I CAN REMEMBER, AND THAT'S A LONG, LONG TIME, THERE ARE ONLY A FEW WAYS OF DOING *IT*, IF YOU GET MY DRIFT. I WAS WONDERING, NOT FOR MYSELF OF COURSE, *ME FORBID,* IF YOU COULD THINK OF ANOTHER

THE ETERNAL SHTUP

WAY OF DOING, *IT*. SO TO RELEIVE THE BORDOM, IF YOU WILL."

Tiffany opened her eyes as wide as she could. She had been asked many questions over the past several hundred years, ever since the time in France when she was with Louis XV and Louis XVI, but no one, not even HIM, had asked if there were other ways of doing *it*. Physiologically, the answer had to be no.

There are only so many things that could be put in only so many places. Everyone knows that.

"May I think about it for a while?"

"TAKE AS MUCH TIME AS YOU LIKE. NO ONE IS GOING ANYWHERE AS FAR AS I KNOW. AND I DO KNOW EVERYTHING."

"With all due respect SIR, there appears to be one thing you do not know. That's my expertise, not yours."

HE had never been spoken to like that before. Of course, she was right. If HE could blush, which he couldn't, he would have.

"HAVE A NICE DAY TIFFANY."

"You too, SIR."

Tiffany wondered, *What other way could there possibly be? And why was HE asking?*

A few hours, or minutes later, she never could be sure, a thought came to her. Something she had not thought about in more than a few hundred years. It was a Chinese, no a Japanese gentleman who had explained it to her. Although she was fascinated by the concept, she was too involved at the time in doing IT the old fashioned way.

I have some research to do.

Tiffany had no lessons in her appointment book, golf or otherwise, so she went to the library. Or the library came to her. It made no difference. She had to satisfy her curiosity.

10

WHAT'S SHE DOING AT THE LIBRARY? WHAT DID I MISS? I KNOW EVERY VOLUMN IN THERE. IT SURE AS HELL WASN'T DEWEY WHO INVENTED THE DECIMAL SYSTEM.

There was always that ethical question HE had to deal with. Was HE spying on his own people and invading their privacy, or in his capacity as HIM, did he have an absolute right to look and listen?

I'LL HAVE TO DUSCUSS THIS WITH ARISTOTLE NEXT TIME I RUN INTO HIM.

HE was sure Tommy Aquinas would argue; he was always arguing; that being The Almighty gave HIM absolute power. How else could HE rule if HE did not posses all the facts? It was never a moral or ethical issue, it was HIS right. One could rightly say, HIS HIM given right.

HE smiled at the pun, but of course totally agreed he was doing nothing wrong. HE also knew there were at least two sides to every argument. It would be only fair, and HE had the well earned reputation of being fair, to allow the other side, in this case, Plato AND Aristotle, an opportunity to rebut Tommy's presumptions.

INTERESTING, VERY INTERESTING.

They never moved, always in the same spot; always wearing the same long robes. They would be filthy by now if it were not for HIM, and the free laundry, dry cleaner and delivery service. As a courtesy they both stopped talking to acknowledge HIS presence. When HE walked over Plato knew the rest of the day would be shot. He did not say what he was thinking. He tried not to even think what he was thinking.

Wouldn't it be great if Leonardo could invent some sort of mind blocking device.

"NO PLATO, IT WOULDN'T."

Someday Plato would learn not to think out loud. Just not today.

HE wasted no time in explaining his dilemma. Did his right, his need to know, usurp what could be interrupted as eaves dropping or invasion of privacy?

Plato pondered the question for a while. He was not prone to giving quick answers. At times he would think about it for days or weeks before responding. He was aware HE wanted an answer, down and dirty, right there and then.

THE ETERNAL SHTUP

"You pose a very interesting question SIR. One that requires a great deal of thought."

"YOU'RE STALLLING PLATO AND WE BOTH KNOW IT. I NEED AN ANSWER AND I NEED IT NOW."

Of course I am stalling. Look who I have to answer to?

"NOT A GREAT ANSWER PLATO. I AM STILL WAITING. AND FOR HEAVENS SAKE, MIND YOUR MANNERS."

Plato was tempted to give HIM the first answer that popped into his mind, but that would not be ethical and if nothing else, Plato was a very ethical person.

When he had to be, Plato was also a practical person. When HE asked him a question, HE expected an answer. Then.

"SIR, the answer is obvious. It is as clear as the sky is blue. When someone says something is their G-d given right, that means exactly what it says. It is a right given by G-d, by YOU. YOU are the only one who can give and take. To do as YOU please. It is your right to listen to your flock. It is your right to watch over your flock. It then stands to reason, a priori, if it is YOUR right, you cannot be guilty of invasion of privacy. Indeed this is YOUR home. We are all guests in YOUR home. YOU have broken no laws, ethical, moral or otherwise."

Plato held his breath, waiting.

"I LIKE YOUR REASONING. I LIKE YOUR ANSWER THOUGH I DO NOT NECESSARILY BELIEVE IT. PERHAPS YOU SHOULD HAVE GONE INTO POLITICS."

"God forbid. Oops. Sorry for that comment SIR. It just came out."

"NO PROBLEM."

HMMM, TWO OPINIONS, SAME ANSWER. I MUST BE RIGHT. WHY SECOND GUESS MYSELF. AFTER ALL, I AM WHO I AM.

While HE was talking to himself, Plato quickly snuck away. Enough philosophy for one day.

Morris stood there absolutely mesmerized.

He had been not five feet away when the conversation had taken place. It was not as if he was eavesdropping, HE had asked Morris to join him at the library. Something about Tiffany looking something up. Trying to find a book, *SHIBUMI*, by Trevanian.

Morris had actually witnessed a conversation, a dialogue, almost an inquisition of one of the greatest philosophers of all time – by HIM.

Amazing.

WHAT COULD BE SO IMPORTANT THAT TIFFANY NEEDED TO READ OR REREAD THIS BOOK?

THE ETERNAL SHTUP

Few people knew Trevanian was a pseudonym for Rodney William Whitaker.

IF MEMORY SERVES ME CORRECTLY, AND IT ALWAYS DOES, THE NOVEL WAS ABOUT NICHOLAI HEI, AN ASSASSIN BORN IN SHANGHAI IN THE EARLY 30'S. 1930's. SOMETIMES I GET MY CENTURYS MIXED UP. AT A VERY EARLY AGE HE LEARNED THE ANCIENT JAPANESE GAME OF GO. HE ALSO LEARNED THE ART OF NAKEDKILL. NICHOLAI HAD THE ABILITY TO MENTALLY ESCAPE FROM REALITY AND COME BACK THOROUGHLY REFRESHED – AND WITH NO GUILT. THE BOOK DELVED IN NICHOLAI'S PRACTICE OF THE ANCIENT ART OF HIGHLY ESOTERIC SEX.

AH, SO THIS IS WHAT TIFFANY WANTS TO RESEARCH. ESOTERIC SEX. BUT WHY? I MUST BE ONE STEP AHEAD OF HER.

While HE was talking to himself, Morris noticed a substantial change in attitude, posture and facial expression. HE apparently was very pleased with himself.

As HE should be.

Morris excused himself. He had just seen Samuel Clements, aka, Mark Twain walking out of the library. He was dying, wrong choice of words, he was most anxious to meet the man who wrote all of his favorite childhood books. He also wanted to see what books he had under his arms.

HE was proficient at many things. Speed reading was just one of them. The occupants were more than mildly surprised when HE picked up a particular book and was on page 146 in a few short minutes. HE slowed down, reread the entire page a few times and put it down.

"THANKS," HE whispered to the flabbergasted librarian. In the more than one hundred forty three and a half years she had been working there, she never heard a thank you from HIM or hardly anyone. Everyone was too busy worrying about themselves.

Everyone thought they owned the place.

HE knew exactly what Tiffany was looking for and would tell him. The ear-to-ear grin could not be mistaken.

HOT DAMN!

When HE was happy, the entire kingdom was happy. UP HERE was indeed HIS kingdom.

11

I need to practice, to understand, to make sure I know what I am talking about before I meet with HIM.

When it came to sex, not a great deal of people knew more, had more hands on experience so to speak, than Tiffany but this was a whole other thing. She decided Morris would be the perfect student. He was always willing to learn. She was sure Veronica would not mind. In fact, she would teach both of them. First one at a time, then maybe both of them together.

They can come together.

Tiff smiled at her play on words.

"Thank you. It was so kind of you to think of us, but Veronica and I have decided to pass."

Morris did not know Veronica overheard every word. Morris was passing up the chance of a lifetime with Tiffany, just to be with her. She was ready to jump his bones, obviously a figure of speech, neither one actually had bones, on the spot.

Tiffany could not believe his words. She was offering a way to experience sex that very few people even knew about and less had tried. And Morris said no. What kind of *schmuck* could he be?

The very thought of esoteric sex blew her mind. She couldn't wait to try it, but like the tango, it took two. Tiff needed a partner, a willing and adventuresome partner and she needed one now. She could say nothing to HIM until she was sure it worked.

Who, who, who?

Tiff was walking aimlessly when she spotted a couple of guys tossing around a football on the new cloud field. She thought she recognized the taller one. Then she was positive she knew both of them. Either one would make a good candidate to use an appropriate figure of speech. The question was, how to approach them.

She knew both brothers took the direct approach and made no bones about what they wanted. They both had a reputation for wanting sex. The more, the better. Tiff decided she had nothing to lose. The taller one was retrieving the football thrown over his head by his younger and small brother.

Tiff approached him.

THE ETERNAL SHTUP

"Excuse me Mr. President. I have an interesting proposition for you, if you have a minute to listen."

JFK was always willing to listen to a proposition from a well built and beautiful young thing.

"Bobby, come on over. This charming young lady has some sort of proposition for me. Maybe for both of us"

He turned to Tiffany who already knew she had hooked a big one.

"We are team players. I hope whatever you have in mind includes my little brother."

It did not take long for Bobby to push his hair away from his eyes so he could get a better look at what he was getting himself into. She did not have the chest of Marilyn, but then, who did. The brothers were immediately thinking threesome. Certainly not the first time, hopefully far from the last.

Jack took off his sweater, spread it on the cloud and asked Tiffany to have a seat. They had all the time in the world to talk. Especially if it was about sex.

Tiff sat down, her short white golf skirt rode up and both boys were immediately interested. It was Jack who was staring at the outline of her nipples and doing a mental comparison. More like several comparisons, like listing them on a chart by size. Ms. M always and all ways, topped the list.

Twenty minutes later the boys laid back and thought about what they were told. It was new, it was novel and it was exciting. It was just not for Jack.

"Bobby, this is not my cup of tea. Too much cerebral and not enough physical. You were always the one with the brains in the family. This should be right up you alley."

Bobby brushed another lock of hair away so he could look deep into Tiff's eyes. He was trying to size her up.

That body could kill me if I am not careful.

Then he remembered, Sirhan Sirhan had already done that, close to fifty years ago.

"I think it is worth talking about. Are we about finished here Jack?"

"Enjoy yourself little brother. Don't do anything I wouldn't do."

All three of them laughed. There was absolutely nothing JFK would not do or had not done.

"I was told you were a man of few words. Do you want me to explain again what I have in mind or do you want to fuck me first?"

"Fuck you first. In the traditional way."

A man after my own heart.

THE ETERNAL SHTUP

Bobby had no idea where they were, not that it mattered. Throwing the pigskin around had warmed up his body. Now he was about to work the other parts of it. They would talk afterwards.

HE was enjoying the view.

SOME PEOPLE JUST NEVER CHANGE.

12

The experiment worked to perfection. As good a body as RFK had, and he did, he had a better brain. He understood exactly what Tiffany had told him. There was no need for explanations or repeating herself.

Being the gentleman his father had taught him to be, he thanked her profusely.

She was now ready to explain everything to HIM.

What she did not know was, HE already knew but had to give credit where credit was due.

IT'S GOOD TO BE ME.

No one had the nerve to argue with that pronouncement.

"SIR, may I have a word with you?"

"OF COURSE, I HAVE BEEN EXPECTING YOU MY DEAR.

THE ETERNAL SHTUP

HE was in a rather generous and joyful mood. He knew what she was about to tell him.

"I promised you an answer but needed to be sure, to test out my theory so to speak, before bringing it to you."

"AND WAS IT SUCCESSFUL"

"Oh, yes Sir."

"AND WAS BOBBY SATISFIED?"

Tiffany felt all the air escape from her little balloon. Her eyes looked straight down and she wanted to yell at HIM.

All my time, effort and work, it was not really work; down the crapper.

HE read her thoughts.

"THAT WAS NOT NICE OF ME. I APOLOGIZE. AS YOU KNOW, I AM THE ALL KNOWING ONE."

"Then I guess I don't have to waste your valuable time explaining the theory. Obviously you already know. I certainly hope you enjoyed watching us, Sir."

"WATCH IT YOUNG LADY. I SAID I WAS SORRY. NOT SOMETHNG YOU HEAR FROM ME EVERYDAY. I WOULD NOT PUSH THE ENVELOPE ANYMORE IF I WERE YOU."

Tiffany immediately regretted what she just said. She had not been thinking. She had forgotten who she was talking to.

"I am so sorry. Please forgive me. May I go now?"

"YES, AND THANK YOU FOR YOUR EFFORT."

The pleasure was all mine. And Bobby's.

"Well?"

"You wouldn't believe it, Jack."

"Don't just stand there with that shit eating grin on your face. Was she as good as, well as . . ."

Here JFK stopped and thought. There had been so many, so very, very many.

"Better."

"Sit. That's an order."

For the next half hour, Jack kept interrupting him with questions, Bobby went through the drill, detail for detail.

"Tell me again, how did it feel? Would you do it again?"

"In a heartbeat. Especially with Tiff."

THE ETERNAL SHTUP

Jack sat there wondering, *Did I make a mistake? Should I have gone instead of Bobby?*

"IT'S NEVER TOO LATE TO FIND OUT JACK."

"Bobby, did you get her phone number?"

"There are no phones up here big brother. She's the head golf pro. She's at the driving range every day. Next time I run into her I'll mention you may be interested. Now why don't you take a nap, Jack."

HE felt it might be a good idea to pass along to Morris what was now rapidly spreading around the neighborhood. Jack was never very good at keeping secrets. Why every Secret Service agent in Washington had a notebook with code names for all of POTUS's girlfriends. The president of the United States loved to tell war stories, clearly not about PT 109, to those who swore to lay down their lives for him. He knew some of the stories had gotten back to Lynden who was stuck with good old Ladybird. This gave Jack a great sense of joy. Now LBJ rarely hung out with any of his old cronies. He spent his spare time, everything UP HERE was spare time, riding his horses.

Horses were only permitted on the south acreage. Technically it was not part of UP HERE. It was a dozen or so clouds over. It took the wink of an eye to get there.

In less than twenty four hours or what JFK thought was a full day, he had discreetly mentioned to Dean Rusk. Bob

McNamara, Abe Ribicoff and Arthur Goldberg, a good part of his old cabinet, what Bobby had done.

And with who.

In all fairness to Rusk, Ribicoff and Goldberg, it was only McNamara, Secretary of Defense under JFK and Johnson, who showed any interest at all in Bobby's adventures. He mentioned he had a nine handicap. Not for one minute did anyone believe him. He was a typical politician. Always trying to screw someone on their own dime.

Within days, Tiffany was the most popular golf instructor UP HERE. Everyone wanted to have her look at their putters and hopefully long drivers. Tiff always wanted to know what type of shaft was attached to the head. And how flexible it was.

HE was upset. This was not to be gutter talk or neighborhood gossip. HE would have a talk with Jack. Soon. In the meantime, he wanted to talk to Morris.

"THERE IS ANOTHER WAY. IT HAS BEEN AUTHENTICATED BY TIFFANY, AT MY REQUEST. MAY I SUGGEST YOU STOP BY AND LET HER KNOW YOU ARE INTERESTED. AND TELL HER WE BOTH APPRECIATE HER TIME AND EFFORT."

"Ah, ah, yes Sir."

Morris was in a state of shock. For two reasons. First, why would HE care about me and my happiness and second, why would HE research such a little unknown piece of information.

"FIRSTLY, BECAUSE I CARE. BECAUSE I CARE ABOUT YOU, MORRIS. SECONDLY, THAT'S MY OWN BUSINESS."

Morris still did not understand. He was one of many. And he still didn't know the secret. Perhaps HE was right. Maybe it was time to take another golf lesson.

"NOT PERHAPS MORRIS. TRUST ME, I AM RIGHT. DO IT, NOW."

Morris smiled. He was already on his way to find the driving range. Or more likely, the driving range would find him.

13

"I'm sorry. For some strange reason Tiffany seems to be booked for, well almost forever."

Morris thanked the assistant head pro. He was not surprised.

"Can you leave her a message?"

Morris and the assistant were both pleasantly surprised when they heard Tiffany's voice behind them. Like she just dropped in from nowhere.

"Hi Morris. What brings you here? Did you suddenly change your mind?"

"Not really. I was sent here. By HIM. And HE said to tell you, HE appreciated your time and effort."

The assistant, who had heard more than he was comfortable knowing, remembered he had a lesson with Payne Stewart. The pro was not sure who was the teacher and who was the student. It didn't matter. He needed to get the hell out of there. The less he heard, the better.

I've got to stop using that word, 'Hell'

"GOOD IDEA GENE. "

Eugenio Sarazen did not have to be told twice. He also didn't want to lose the best gig he had in the last seventeen years. Assistant pro UP HERE was better than when he won the Masters in '35 and the U. S. Open in 1922 and 32.

"So HE sent you. Do you want the lesson?"

"I'm not sure 'want' is the right word. I 'need' to learn. HE needs me to learn."

"No time like the present."

Before Morris could say, 'Where', they were in a cottage. Morris looked around. They were alone. Completely alone.

"Sit over there. You may look; I want you to look, but no touching. None."

Morris heard what she said but clearly did not understand. They were there to have sex. Sex is all about touching and a whole lot more.

"Now close your eyes and think about what it is like to slowly undress me. Don't actually do it, just think it."

Morris did as he was told. He felt he was getting excited.

"Please describe to me every bit of intimate apparel you are removing from my sensual body and how you are feeling about it."

Strangely enough, for the first time in more than two hundred forty years, Tiffany was wearing undergarments. A front hook, pink lace bra and matching silk panties. She also had on a shocking pink garter belt - but no stockings.

Morris nodded.

"When can we actually do it?"

The question was more like a plea. A plea of a man in the desert who thirsted for a taste of spring water.

"That's the whole point. We never actually touch each other. It is called esoteric love making. Some would call it mind fucking, not a term HE's terribly fond of. The purpose is to excite your partner to the point of orgasm, without any physical contact. Whoever comes first, loses. It is a great exercise when you are in a room with others or want to experience the ultimate love making when your physical surroundings make it impossible. Still want to play?"

Morris nodded his head again. His mind was in a whirl.

"Your Eminence, your three o'clock appointment has been waiting for more than fifteen minutes."

THE ETERNAL SHTUP

"GO AWAY. CANCEL THE APPOINTMENT OR RESCHEDULE. I'M BUSY. PLEASE DON'T BOTHER ME UNTIL I BUZZ YOU. UNDERSTOOD?"

"Yes Your Eminence."

HE was on the edge of his seat, figuratively speaking. HE was hanging on every word between Morris and Tiff. For someone who had seen it all, HE was fascinated. HE did not want to miss a single word. Or gesture. HE could not wait to see how it ended.

"Now picture you fondling me. How do my breasts feel? How do my nipples feel? Do you want to touch or suck? Or both?"

Morris was having a difficult time. His breathing was becoming heavy and his hands were trembling. Any thought of Veronica or fidelity were now long gone.

"Both."

"I will wait until you are satisfied, then we can move on."

Morris was more than ready to move on.

"Wait, I have forgotten something. The most important part. They whole purpose of this exercise. I want you to excite me. Stop concentrating on pleasuring yourself and say anything you can, to get me to come."

Morris was unable to stop what he was thinking. He was so close. And now Tiff wanted him to concentrate on pleasing her. He was not sure he could do it.

HE could not stop watching. It was the most exciting thing to happen since Rosemary's baby tried to get in and was summarily refused. Peter had done his job and done it well. HE turned his head slightly to get a better angle and not miss a word.

FASINATING. TRULY FASINATING.

HE was speaking to no one. Just expressing HIS thoughts

Morris was new at this. He had never had to worry about the girl coming. That was her problem. He had always been selfish. Now for probably the first time, he understood the meaning of pleasing each other. Coming together.

Morris began to make some remarks about his hard, strong penis. He was totally unconvincing. He wanted to sexually excite Tiffany but all the time he was only thinking of himself.

The hell with winning the game. All I want to do is come.

WATCH YOUR LANGUAGE MORRIS.

Tiffany sensed what he was thinking and wanted to postpone it. HE knew exactly what Morris was thinking and was disappointed. HE had expected more from him.

MAYBE NEXT TIME.

THE ETERNAL SHTUP

There was no question; there would be a next time.

Tiffany was not ready to give up. She was the teacher and knew Rome was not built in a day, at least not according to HIM. She would allow him to lose the first game and maybe give him more incentive to try again.

"You are now ready to enter me. I am wet and waiting. I desire you more than any man I ever wanted before."

Morris was about to make a comment when he let out a low, guttural groan.

"I'm coming!"

From the look on his contorted face, no explanation was necessary. Morris then looked embarrassed and sheepish. He had come and he had lost.

"Morris, the object of this exercise is to learn self-restraint. Control. To concentrate on pleasuring your partner, not yourself, first. I appreciate this was only your first lesson. You need practice, lots of practice."

Morris was about to reply but Tiff was now gone. She had simply vanished. Morris knew what he had to do. And with whom.

"IS MY THREE O'CLOCK STILL WAITING?"

"He really has nowhere else to go Your Eminence."

HE had cleared his mind but knew the next Morris episode would come shortly. HE would keep HIS eyes and ears open.

"SEND HIM IN."

Morris had no idea how long he slept. When he woke, Veronica was quietly doing a crossword puzzle. She had a smile on her face.

"Well, tell me all about it."

"You know?"

"Of course I know. How many times do I have to tell you? There are no secrets here."

Morris was almost afraid to face her.

"Tell me exactly what I should do. I can't wait for us to practice."

"Yes dear," Morris answered.

14

To say HE was a great multi-tasker, would be a gross understatement. Keeping track of Morris was only one of the things on HIS mind. There were hundreds, if not thousands. Truly it was a thankless job. But as the old joke goes, "Someone has to do it."

The three o'clock appointment did not begin to close to four. The four was pushed back to four thirty and all others were rescheduled. Talk about thankless jobs, being HIS appointment secretary was way up there. At times Judas felt like he was being punished. For what he was not sure. Besides, that incident was more than two thousand years ago.

Judas was eternally sorry for the way it turned out.

I guess I never really thought it through.

"NO YOU DIDN'T. YOU KNEW HE WAS MY SON, DIDN'T YOU?"

Judas didn't want to argue. It was one debate he could never win.

"May we call it a day, SIR?

HE was still in a good mood, thanks to Morris and Tiff. Maybe let bygones be bygones. At least for today.

"WHY DON'T YOU GO OUT AND HAVE SOME FUN – WITH THE OTHER APOSTLES."

"Thank you, Your Eminence. I'll give it a try. I hope the boys are not still mad at me."

"TELL THEM I FORGIVE YOU."

HE had a tough time getting that one out.

Judas felt better.

HE heard familiar voices. They were from Morris and Veronica. Being responsible for their well being, HE felt a moral obligation to take a peek at what they were up to.

"GOOD EVENING JUDAS, YOU MAY LEAVE. I HAVE SOME MORE WORK TO DO. THIS JOB IS NEVER ENDING."

Morris was explaining to Veronica precisely what he had been told. The object was to please your partner before you pleased yourself. There was one rule and one rule only. No touching. Everything else was fair game. Morris already was formulating an idea, a strategy.

THE ETERNAL SHTUP

I WONDER WHAT HIS STRATEGY IS?

You would have thought HE had nothing else to do or it was one of his own children. Technically speaking, they were all HIS children. HE began to wonder to himself why.

WHY AM I TAKING SUCH A KEEN INTEREST? THERE ARE SO MANY MORE PRESSING PROBLEMS FOR ME TO WORRY ABOUT.

HE had again been mulling over the idea of draining the entire Middle East of oil. The problem with that was the entire world, to some extent, depended on that oil. The Arabs would go back to being nomads trading camels for women, but what about countries in the Far East that depended on the precious black gold? What about America that was still not up to speed. Their government had plenty of wind power thanks to Washington the city, not the first president, but that would not help Detroit. Who would the Jews blame for their forever suffering if not the A Rabs?

HAVEN'T THOSE RAGHEADS LEARNED YET? THEY MAY WANT A WOMAN, BUT THEY NEED A CAMEL. IN THE LONG RUN, THEY ARE ALWAYS YOUR BEST BUY.

I GUESS I SHOULDN'T HAVE USED THE WORD,'RAGHEAD'. NOT VERY GODLY OF ME. THEY ARE ALL MY CHILDREN.

At times, even HE had doubts.

HE was now distracted by the comments made by Morris. He was now being the aggressor.

THAT BOY IS SURE ONE FAST LEARNER.

Veronica and Morris were sitting in the living room. On separate chairs, each facing the other. They were no more than four feet apart. Each was making erotic comments and gestures. They each stayed in their own space. It was obvious they were both close to exploding. It was only a matter of who could concentrate the longest. It was a battle of wills. Veronica made a rather lewd suggestion; Morris threw his head back and let out a muffled scream. Veronica was thrilled. Her first time and she had won. To celebrate and because she was so close to losing it also, she too made it known that she just had a giant orgasm.

"Ha, I won."

Veronica had no idea what Morris was talking about.

"I faked it. I didn't come. I just let you believe I did so you would."

With that he let her see what was now happening. He had not lied.

"No fair. You tricked me."

"Yes I did but the game is not over. In fact it has just begun. We have an entire eternity to please each other. Next time, trust but verify."

Veronica was pleased she had lost. It had made Morris happy, and that was all that mattered.

THE ETERNAL SHTUP

HE could not believe what he was seeing and hearing. HE almost fell over laughing.

"HO, HO, HO."

He could have easily been mistaken for elderly, very elderly Santa Clause.

I REALLY SHOULDN'T BE LAUGHING, BUT MORRIS CERTAINLY DID PUT ONE OVER ON HER.

HE was interrupted by a loud knock on his door. HE did not have to ask who it was, he already knew. Manchem Begin and Anwar Sadat were standing outside.

Arguing as usual.

"GENTLEMEN, COME IN. HAVE A SEAT, TAKE A LOAD OFF YOUR FEET. WHAT'S THE PROBLEM THIS TIME?"

HE obviously knew the problem. It never changed. HE considered the old ploy of the oil to see who would blink first. HE already knew Begin's reply.

"If there is water, we will stay. We can live without oil, not without water. This is our homeland. We are going nowhere. So what's next on YOUR agenda?"

HE was looking forward to a quiet night alone, watching Monday Night Football. The New Orleans Saints, his favorite team was playing. There was no question who would win but it was fun to kick back and relax. Just not tonight. The eternal argument with the two former heads of State, was going nowhere.

By the time Begin and Sadat left, the first half of the game had ended. HE watched the throngs of spectators heading for the concession stands and rest rooms. There was every type of food imaginable to purchase and eat. Chile dogs, burgers, Philly cheese steak on a fat roll, popcorn, pretzels, French fries, beer, soda and Gatorade, to mention a few items on the big board above the concession stands. They were stuffing themselves while half the world went to bed on an empty stomach. That brought up the eternal nagging problem of overpopulation and world hunger, two of the biggies on HIS list.

Earth could not keep up with the unchecked population growth in most of Africa and Asia. Parts of the USA, particularly the Deep South, had not accepted the consequences of the problem.

THERE MUST BE AN ANSWER. IT'S AT MY FINGERTIPS, AND YET I CAN'T GRAB IT.

HIS thoughts were interrupted by Veronica and Morris. They were practicing their new found game - again.

THAT'S IT; THAT'S IT.

HE had just experienced a brain fart. In the snap of a finger, Veronica and Morris were standing in front of him. They were fully clothed, naturally, but obviously embarrassed. They had been "caught in the act."

THE ETERNAL SHTUP

"I NEED A FAVOR.

It was rare, very rare; anyone ever heard those words from HIM.

In unison, "Yes SIR."

"HOW WOULD THE TWO OF YOU LIKE TO BE AMBASSADORS OF LOVE?"

Morris and Veronica just looked at each other. They had no idea what HE was talking about.

"IF THIS WORKS, AND IT WILL, I'LL SEND OTHERS. TIFFANY WILL HELP IN MY SELECTION. SHE SEEMS TO HAVE A UNIQUE GIFT FOR WHO WOULD BE BEST QUALIFIED."

Morris again looked at Veronica – and then at HIM.

"HERE IS MY IDEA. TELL ME WHAT DO YOU THINK?"

A half hour later Morris and Veronica were shaking their heads. They supposed it could work. It might just work.

"IT WILL WORK. TRUST ME ON THAT ONE."

The next day or what seemed like the next day, they were all sitting around a conference table on Cloud 3. Naturally, HE was at the head of the table. In addition to Morris and Veronica and Tiffany and RFK, there were two other couples. Ming Haw Sang and his girlfriend Gintasa, both originally from mainland China and Kumbasa Quanza and an absolutely stunning, long legged beauty by the name of Ubangee, from Ghana.

I'M GOING TO HAVE TO CHECK, TO SEE IF THAT'S HER FIRST OR LAST NAME. IN ANY CASE, SHE'S A LOOKER.

"SIR, her last name is Mee."

"THANK YOU PETER. GOOD WORK."

The four couples would make up the initial trial ambassadors. If it worked, and HE knew it would, other couples would be recruited. Eventually there would be hundreds of Ambassadors of Love disbursed to under-developed / over-populated areas of the world. They would teach esoteric love. A method of fulfilling one's self sexually without the consequence of pregnancy and unwanted babies.

"IT'S A BRILLIANT IDEA, IF I MUST SAY SO MYSELF."

No one had the nerve to disagree or even think it.

Morris and Veronica were the first to go. They would be sent to Tupelo, Mississippi. No one had ever been granted, long term, Right of Return. For a long weekend in unusual circumstances. To say goodbye to one who was not coming UP HERE or to finish something that could not be accomplished anywhere but earth.

THE ETERNAL SHTUP

Morris had never been to Tupelo, let alone Mississippi. He had never been to Arkansas, Tennessee, Alabama or any of the Deep South where everyone seemed to be a first cousin to everyone else. Marrying outside the family was almost a sin. It gave new meaning to the term, Kissen Cousins.

Morris was born in The Bronx and retired to southeast Florida. He had never been exposed to those people. Why Tupelo was the birthplace of Elvis. That should tell you something.

Perhaps I should have a talk with Mr. Presley.

Morris knew he was Up Here. He had a feeling Elvis would not be a strong proponent of sex without touching. The whole idea of sex was to get down and dirty, to grunt and groan. To sweat and work it. To actually spread those little seeds of life. To bust that damn egg like a riff from an electric StratoCruiser while throwing out his exaggerated pelvis.

Morris was shocked. Elvis looked to be no more than twenty one, twenty two at the most. His hair was slicked back in a D.A., hips constantly moving and a sly twinkle in his eyes. He knew he was destined for greatness, he just did not know someday he would be The King.

"Don't know nuthin about that stuff. We are pretty fond of the old fashioned way. Bin working for years, I guess forever. Sure be obliged to help you though. Whatever HE wants."

Morris was fascinated by some of the stories he was told. Did young boys really learn from sheep and farm animals or was Elvis just putting him on.

ELVIS DOES NOT LIE. AT LEAST NOT UP HERE, MORRIS. BESIDES, IF THE SHEEP DOESN'T LIKE IT, SHE CAN AWAYS SAY 'NA'.

HE then laughed loudly at his own joke.

15

'I'M NOT SURE HOW LONG YOUR RIGHT OF RETURN WILL LAST. YOU KNOW I WILL BE WATCHING AND LISTENING. ASK QUESTIONS, TALK TO ME ANYTIME, DAY OR NIGHT. NOT THAT THERE'S ANY DIFFERENCE."

Before Morris could answer he found himself in front of Cookie's Diner on Robert E. Lee Avenue in downtown Tupelo. He was wearing denim coveralls, work boots and a Mississippi State baseball type hat. He was a mite grungy and had not shaved in a day or two. Veronica was wearing a gingham dress down to her ankles and now had her hair in pigtails. They were both around thirty years old, no longer youngins. Morris had no idea what to do or say – or who to say it to.

"Welcome strangers. You both look lost and could use a good meal."

Morris had an urge to tell the big guy with a tattered straw hat and a chaw of tobacco in his cheek, he had not had a morsel of food in days or weeks or months.

Veronica had not had a meal in more than a few dozen years.

"Be right pleased to have you as my guests. Names Jethro. Jethro Presley. Bin mayor here for nigh on thirty-five years. Ever since my second cousin put Tupelo on the map. He sure was one of those good ol' boys who never forgot where his roots were.

Morris had the distinct feeling that running into Elvis's cousin was not a coincidence. He never believed in coincidences.

"Thank you Mr. Mayor."

"No need for formality here. Just you call me Jethro like everyone else does. Hope you guys like grits. You're standing in front of the best place in the county for them. What brings you good folks to our neck of the woods?"

Veronica hesitated. Morris was tongue tied. Finally his mouth began to relax and work.

"We have been sent by HIM. We are Ambassadors of Love. We are here to educate the good people of Earth."

Morris looked upwards as he pronounced the word HIM with emphasis.

Jethro thought he had heard it all. This was a new one. He wondered how much it would cost the town before he had to run them out.

THE ETERNAL SHTUP

"NOT ONE RED CENT. TRUST HIM JETHRO. BY THE WAY, YOUR NEW CALF IS NOW DOING JUST FINE, THANKS TO ME. YOUR COUSIN ELVIS ASKED ME TO TELL YOU THAT OLD STRATOCRUISER, THE ONE HE USED TO RECORD JAILHOUSE ROCK, THE ONE YOU HAVE BEEN SEARCHING FOR THE LAST TWENTY FIVE YEARS IS OVER AT COUSIN CLEM'S. IN THE BARN LOFT WRAPPED UP IN AN OLD ARMY BLANKET WAY IN THE BACK. HALF THE PROCEEDS FROM THE SALE SHOULD GO TO BUILD THE NEW CHURCH YOU BEEN THINKING ABOUT."

A look of fear, surprise and respect immediately crossed Jethro's weather-lined face. He was positive he had just heard the word of G-d. And he had.

"YES SIR."

"Whatever you good folks want, all you need to do is ask. I'd be most pleased to allow you to use the church as a meeting hall for as long as you need it. Come' on. Time for y'all to have some down home cookin."

16

In the Province of Wuhan, China, Ming Haw and Gintasa were standing on the street in traditional dress wondering how they had been given the unprecedented Right of Return. They knew their mission and how HE would guide them, even if it were temporary only.

Unknown to them, a town hall meeting had been called. All had been invited to attend. No one was sure who called the meeting, what it was about or why attendance, though not mandatory, it was strongly suggested. The speakers were to be Ming Haw and Gintasa. This was to be an ADULTS ONLY meeting. Ming and Gintasa had no idea what they would say, how they would say it or what the reaction would be. Being run out of town seemed like the most likely scenario. They had not counted on the influence of HIM. No one could have accurately anticipated how HIS percussion would dramatically change the outcome.

It was agreed RFK and Tiffany, billed as Bobby and Tiff, would be Ambassadors at Large. It was what Bobby had always hoped and prayed for. They would have no specific territory and would go where they were most needed. Today it could be Caracas, Venezuela, tomorrow, Sapporo, Japan and the next day Moscow. They needed no planes, no hotel reservations and carried no luggage. It was the only way to travel.

Bobby loved every minute of it.

For the first time in centuries, Tiffany was excited. No more boring golf lessons. No more practicing grips and swings and positioning of the hips. She was now spreading the word. And nothing else. Bobby was a born B. S. artist or as he preferred to be known, an accomplished orator. He was born not only to debate and convince, but to lead. Had his life not ended in the kitchen of that L A hotel, he could have been one of the great ones. Probably not the most loved, but that was never his goal. From his very first memories, he was born to lead. Born to make a difference. This was now his chance for eternity. To be known as Robert F. Kennedy, not Jack's kid brother.

"Would you like to practice some more, just so if anyone asks questions, we both know the answers."

Bobby smiled. "I have always been a student of perfection. Knowledge is power."

Bobby knew he would be facing a tough crowd tonight for their presentation. They would be in the Mormon Tabernacle in downtown Salt Lake City. The wives outnumbered the husbands seven to one. Just about the normal ratio for Mormons. The husbands were all there under duress but were told it was the express wish of the late, great Brigham Young for them to attend. No one could rightfully refuse. They would listen but that was it. No one could tell them what to do or more important, how to do it.

Bobby was relying heavily on Tiff. She had proven time and time again, to be most persuasive. It remained to be seen how persuasive she really was.

HE was keeping close attention to all HIS ambassadors – and the results they were achieving. If the results were up to HIS expectations, the number of ambassadors would be substantially expanded.

THEY WILL BE. I HAVE ORDAINED IT.

Tiff and Bobby seemed to be having the best results. HE was sure it was not the location chosen or the charisma of Kennedy but clearly the special talents of Tiffany. She had insisted one can never dismiss an idea before trying it. There had to have been twenty three hundred Mormon men who agreed to the experiment. While the wives watched in amazement, all twenty three hundred tried their hardest to bring Tiffany to orgasm by wishing it with all their minds and energy. Tiff did likewise in not such ladylike language. In the end, the solution was obvious. The men would have applauded, but that was quite impossible, under the circumstances.

Tiff singlehandedly, made progress.

THE ETERNAL SHTUP

HE knew it would take years and years to evaluate the progress. HE also knew time was inconsequential. A few hundred years was a mere drop in the bucket. All HE really was looking for was change. A reversal of the trend.

TIME IS ON MY SIDE; TIME IS ALWAYS ON MY SIDE.

Word of the Right of Return project quickly spread throughout the Kingdom. Casual side bets were made by Socrates and Nero; among others. The old timers were betting No. Man has always been a sensuous individual. One who always demands pleasure from every sense, from every source, from every orifice. While the mind must always be stimulated, if other parts of the body were denied, there would be blood running in the streets. The proletariat would rebel. Together with the French, (before they were invaded by the Muslims) the Bolsheviks in Russia would never allow it.

Tommy Aquinas had all his money, not that he ever acquired much for a lifetime of work, on the side of The Almighty. The old time philosophers never gave enough credit to *Man and his Mind*. Surely they will see and understand the need for the common good.

HE was displeased at the big Vegas style board that was set up to record the odds as they constantly changed based upon earthly results. Each team on Earth had their own odds. Besides the Vegas brokers there were a group of former Chinese War Lords accepting big bets. There was a certain excitement not normally found in such a peaceful place. The upside, if there was one, HE realized a tremendous amount of interest and energy was being generated. As usual, it was HIS doings.

The fourth couple, Kumbasa Quanza and his long legged companion Ubangee were making no progress at all. Between blood diamonds that controlled the lives of those in Ghana and the threat of Ebola from neighboring countries, the citizens had no time for such nonsense. They were refused meeting halls and no one would talk to them. Life was a constant struggle. HE was fully aware of the problem.

I NEED A HOOK. SOMETHING TO GET THEIR ATTENTION. FIRST IT WAS AIDS, THEN EBOLA. THE LAST THING ON THEIR MINDS IS NONE-TOUCHING SEX. THEY NEED SOMETHING TO LOOK FOREWARD TO.

He decided to have a quiet talk with Tommy Jefferson. He knew what was best for the people and had more than a passing acquaintance with how blacks thought and reacted. After all, several of his own children were black.

"No one appreciates what they have, till they lose it. Find something they cherish, take it away from them and then if they are good and cooperate, give it back to them. It's sort of like freedom."

HE listened to Tom Terrific and had to agree with him. After all, the man did write the Declaration of Independence, was one of America's founding fathers, the first Secretary of State under old 'wooden choppers' George, U.S. Minister to France where he got into all sorts of compromising situations and finally the third president of the United States. The man did have some fairly strong credentials. Now he mostly sat around wondering how Virginia's football team was doing and constantly arguing with Madison and Monroe.

At times he could not let well enough alone.

'ANY SUGGESTIONS TOM?"

"Take away and then give back. But what," Tommy answered.

Ghana's most valuable asset was of course, their land. The land that produced gold, diamonds and oil. The population was more than twenty seven million and growing every day, every hour. There were no shortages of babies, only the resources to keep them alive.

"What if it is suggested that once the population reaches thirty million, and it will in a year or two, the country will be split in two. Half would go to the Ivory Coast that is just itching to get their hands on the gold and blood diamonds and the other half goes Nigeria to the south?

HE thought about it without giving an answer.

Jefferson continued.

"We don't really take anything away. We, I mean the United Nations or the Federation of African States, just threatens. That would cause a drop in the birth rate in a heartbeat. My guess is Kumbasa and Ms. Mee would be welcomed with open arms."

Old Silver Tongue Tom could tell he was getting through.

"LET ME THINK ABOUT IT."

Tom knew it was now all but a done deal.

JFK was not in a great mood. He was complaining his back was bothering him – again. He failed to mention he was not particularly pleased Bobby was now getting all the attention.

After Joe Jr. died in The War, it was John or Jack as his close friends called him, who always got what he wanted, starting with that cute little Enquiring Reporter, Jackie Bouvier. A real gold digger that charm-your-pants-off with that phony innocence, slut. According to Aristotle, the ship builder, not the philosopher, he grossly overpaid for what he contracted for.

From commander of PT 109 to member of the House of Representatives for the 11th Congressional District of Massachusetts to Senator from Massachusetts to defeating *Tricky Dick* to become the 35th president of the United States. He had it all till that fateful ride in Dallas in November, 1963.

Never trust a Lincoln.

Jack was thinking of the car he was in when he made his final waive, not the six foot four, sixteenth president of the USA.

Now Bobby was the At Large, Ambassador for Love. RFK was news, big news. Jack sat in his rocking chair trying to remember all the women the Secret Service snuck into the White House. That would keep him busy for a while.

When is it my turn?

There are no special favors, president or not. JFK was just another has been. HE was not about to make any exceptions. Richard Millhouse Nixon was just waiting to pounce if HE did. Even UP THERE, *Tricky Dick* still could not stand the sight of *Smiling Jack*.

Those damn TV lights at the debate and me sweating like a stuffed pig, ruined me. I knew jack shit about cameras and lights and all that crap. If there was a crook in the White House, it wasn't me.

"Sir, how can I help; what can I do?"

HE knew this was coming. Jack hated to be on the outside – of anything.

"PATIENCE JACK, FOR MY SAKE, PATIENCE,"

The former president was not used to being spoken to like that. He decided to look up his old Mafia girlfriend. She would keep him company or at least his mind occupied for a few hours.

I work my backside off and Bobby has all the fun. I never should have shared Marilyn (or all those others) with him.

It did not take long for word to spread. Jethro's bull calf, on death's door twenty four hours ago, was now standing on his four legs and nursing like there was no end of milk in sight. As to Elvis's old guitar, it was wrapped in an army blanket under a pile of rags in the back of the loft of Cousin Clem's barn.

Just like HE promised.

After all these years it was still in perfect shape. The guitar would be sold by Sotheby's and the profits split down the middle. Half for the new church and half to the mayor. One would have thought it was a miracle.

Jethro made no bones about it. It was indeed the word of HIM.

That evening Morris and Veronica spoke to a SRO crowd at the old church. When Veronica announced she would be pleased to give private instructions to all who were serious, you would have thought she was giving away bales of tobacco. Or maybe a few kilos of weed. The next day a second, third and fourth town meeting was scheduled. No one wanted to miss a word. After all, this was practically the gospel from THE MAN himself. The fact Veronica was HIS messenger did not hurt the attendance.

HE was pleased. It was all going according to plan.

NOW TO CHECK ON THE OTHERS.

17

"I HAVE A REAL CHALLENGE FOR YOU. EVEN WITH MY HELP I AM NOT SURE THE TWO OF YOU CAN PULL IT OFF. HAVE A SEAT. THIS COULD TAKE A WHILE."

Bobby and Tiff had just come back from a four day stint in Bombay. If they could make a dent in India, anything was possible. They could not build enough schools or computers to handle the demand. The job opportunities at Verizon, Comcast and Best Buy, were overwhelming. Every American company needed techs that were computer savvy and had a vague concept of how to speak English, as spoken in the USA.

Having babies was a national pastime in India and yet with HIS help, the meeting halls were full with interested and upward mobile young listeners.

What could be worse than India, Tiffany thought.

"I'LL TELL YOU WHAT COULD BE WORSE. NEW CITY, NEW YORK IN ROCKLAND COUNTY. IT'S THE HOME OF MORE

THAN 10,000 CRAZY, FANATICAL MESHUGANAH, HASSIDIC JEWS. THEY PROBABLY THINK NEW CITY IS AN ORTHODOX SUBURB OF JERUSALEM."

RFK and Tiffany looked at HIM. They needed to know more. A lot more. New City was less than 20 miles from New York City. The population was just over 36,000. For reasons unknown to anyone, well almost anyone, many Hassidic Jews were tired of living in the Williamsburg section of Brooklyn. They moved upstate and began buying everything in sight. Homes, businesses, whatever was for sale. If it was not for sale, an exorbitant offer suddenly made it available. The old time residents were not pleased.

Not by a long shot.

The way to take over a city, town, state or country was by population growth. Look at the problems London, Paris and Jerusalem are having with the Arab / Muslim population. They populate like rabbits. He, who controls the votes, controls the government. In twenty years the Muslims in many countries in Europe will outnumber the original residents. Then they steal the elections – legal like. In less than ten years more than fifty percent of voters in New City will be Hassidic Jews.

This was not good for anyone.

Bobby was impressed. Boston was mostly populating Irish Catholics. The Pope had never told his father Joe, the ramifications of that little secret.

THE ETERNAL SHTUP

"What do you want us to do? Do YOU have a plan Sir?"

Bobby was always respectful when talking to someone with power. Who could possibly have more power than HIM?

"NOT YET, BUT I WILL. BOTH OF YOU, WEAR BLACK. CONSERVATIVE BLACK. AND TIFFANY, NO SKIN SHOWING. PLEASE."

Tiff blushed. She could forget her new robe, the one with a slit almost to her thigh. She wondered if she had to wear a *burka*.

"NO. AND DON'T BE A SMART ASS. THIS IS SERIOUS STUFF. REMEMBER, IT'S MY REPUTATION ON THE LINE."

Tiffany lowered her eyes as if to apologize.

Arch Bishop Francis Joseph Spellman would not have recognized Bobby if he were standing on top of him. He had on a long black coat, a wrinkled and ill fitting suit and an ultra wide black hat. The fact he was clean shaven and had no *paepes,* were the only giveaway. Tiffany, with her hair hidden, could have been his younger sister.

They still needed bait. HE promised he would provide.

While they waited, Tiff suggested a bite to eat. Bobby was not sure if eating was permitted. He too was hungry. Sol Cohen's Kosher Deli was around the corner. They could both smell the aroma drifting into their nostrils.

"GO. ENJOY. STUFF YOUR FACES BUT REMEMBER, IT'S LIKE KISSING A NUN. IT'S O.K TO HAVE A TASTE BUT JUST DON'T GET IN THE HABIT."

HE was now chuckling. HE had made another joke.

HIS other favorite was told to him by his old buddy, Confucius.

"What kind of meat does a priest eat on Friday?"

"Nun."

HE did not know whether to laugh or cry at that one.

Bobby and Tiffany had already been seated. Tiff almost began to drool as she read the menu.

They both ordered the same appetizer, homemade chicken soup with two large fluffy matzo balls. It was delicious. If either of them had a Jewish grandmother, it would have been a major competition. Neither obviously did.

They scoured the menu as if it were their last supper. Bobby immediately gravitated to the corned beef and cabbage with boiled potatoes and vegetables. It was not what was served back in Hyannis Port. But it was solid, that's really all he cared about.

Tiff had no idea when her next meal would be, if ever, and agonized between the grilled liver and onions with mashed potatoes and the beef brisket platter. As the old time waiter chewed his pencil and looked mildly annoyed, Tiff finally went for the brisket with crisp potato pancakes topped with apple sauce.

To use a totally inappropriate cliché, it was to die for.

The waiter could not believe they practically licked their plates clean. As if they had not eaten in weeks – or in their case, decades.

HE observed the entire meal, beginning to end and thought he was getting more than a twinge of hunger pains.

IMPOSSIBLE, THOUGH THE LATKES, FRIED POTATO PANCAKES LOOKED AND SMELLED DELICIOUS.

HE now had work to do. A plan. A plan that would look like HE was doing them a big favor while in reality, actually asking for one. HE also decided he would ask for help. Not many people realized rabbis and leaders of non Christian religions were admitted to the Kingdom of Heaven. HE had his choice of some of the greats and near greats.

WHO DO I CALL FIRST?

HE was momentarily distracted. It seems what had begun as a discussion became an argument and finally ended up in an honest-to-HIM-brawl. Martin Luther King had been dead since the 1960's. Governor George Corley Wallace from the great State of Alabama had survived an assassination attempt in 1972 that left him paralyzed and extremely bitter.

"It was all because he refused to stay where he belonged."

Wallace died in 1998 and blamed MLK every waking minute of his life since he became chained to his damn wheelchair.

More than a few people were surprised the Southern populist and true segregationist ever made it ALL THE WAY UP. The two of them had avoided each other for years but it was inevitable someday they would cross paths. King, being the pacifist, avoided the bully at all costs.

When push came to shove, and it did, both men used every dirty method they knew. It was a true no-holds-barred donnybrook.

OY VEY. I THOUGHT THIS WAS SUPPOSED TO BE MY KINGDOM.

18

Kennedy and Tiff were temporarily forgotten.

Christmas was just around the corner. It was a difficult time of year for HIM. HE tried to play no favorites.

There were Christmas trees and Hanukkah bushes. There were little angels and menorahs everywhere. Some gifts were wrapped in red and gold; others with blue and white ribbons. And that was just the beginning. Then there was Kwanzaa. Fortunately there were no department stores or Hallmark card gift shops; there was no Black Friday, Cyber Monday or Return Everything Wednesday. There were no Before Christmas or After Christmas sales. There were no credit cards or layaways. There was also no cookies or pecan pies or schnitzel and noodle. There were no Mad Avenue executives or wall-to-wall media advertising on TV and newspapers. It was a religious time of year, not a mass marketing ploy.

SORT OF WHAT I ORGINALLY HAD IN MIND.

There was also no snow. Or eggnog or mistletoe. There were also no last minute Amazon and Fed Ex deliveries.

Like a flash, the thought came to HIM.

IT WAS ALL BECAUSE HE REFUSED TO STAY WHERE HE BELONGED.

Those were Wallace's exact words. And everyone knew what happened next. The South, in fact the entire country would never be the same again. All because Marty believed all men were created equal. Not only before the eyes of the law but at luncheon counters in Selma and Birmingham. In fact, all over the Deep South. Fortunately time, circumstances and the Kennedy Brothers were Johnny-on-the-spot. It was time to make history, to solve the social inequalities of a new nation, to right the unspeakable wrong, to dream the impossible dream.

KING REFUSED TO STAY WHERE HE BELONGED.

HE thought about that phrase. It could be the key to resolving the problem in New City. First there would be a series of quiet conversations to test the waters. Then Bobby and Tiff could be given their marching orders. All of a sudden, HE was very proud of what he was doing.

There were still a few businesses and single family homes for sale in New City. In a matter of days all were purchased. No contingencies. Cash only. No one knew who the new owners were. Apparently it was an off shore corporation or family trust. The attorneys were purposely vague, still a certified check was all the sellers needed to see and know.

Within thirty days every single piece of real estate was sold. No negotiations. Then the surprise came. All buyers were African Americans. Every last one of them. The Hasidic community was in a mild uproar. This was their town. They did not want it integrated.

By anyone!

There was not much they could do. The law was the law.

Enter the former Attorney General of the United States of America. The Most Honorable Robert F. Kennedy. It was decided the initial meetings with the new town fathers would be one-on-one. Off the record. Tiffany would be brought in later. She carried the big guns, the big bazookas.

Quid pro quo. Latin for *'You scratch my back, I'll scratch yours'.*

It was tactfully suggested, by the most astute politician, that the new trend could continue, fair market value was not a serious consideration; the buyer had as much money as HIM, really a misconception as to HIS wealth, or the trend could be reversed, depending on how amenable they were to listening to new ideas on birth control.

At first there was a Mexican standoff.

"No one tells us what to do," stated Rabbi Schumer.

Then the word came down. THE COMPANY would buy any property in New City for one hundred thirty five percent of assessed value. More than a few Hassidic businessmen suddenly had a yearning to return to the good old days in the Williamsburg section of Brooklyn.

There was an old expression, the origination of which was frankly unknown,

MONEY TALKS, BULLSHIT WALKS.

Thirty five percent profits certainly was not bull shit.

The talks began in earnest. Progress was slow at first. Very slow. Then Ms. Tiffany was snuck in the back door. She made an impression. She made a difference. The wives were pleased. The midwives were not. No woman should have the burden, regardless of their religious beliefs, to have to carry eight to ten children and in some cases, twelve to fifteen, or until they were unable to conceive anymore.

HE was very pleased.

ALL'S WELL THAT ENDS WELL.

HE was quoting one of his old friends, really not that old, who he spoke to often, Wee Willy Shakespeare.

After less than six weeks Bobby and Tiff were given a new assignment. Bobby had put on close to twenty pounds and was not fit for even tag football. His new nickname could have been Pudge.

THE ETERNAL SHTUP

Tiffany, bless her heart, and HE did, could have used the added support of a new bra; she did not own an old one.

None of the adult male residents seemed to mind.

She had potato pancakes with sour cream or apple sauce, almost every day. She didn't even have to order. The waiters knew and were happy to oblige – and openly stared at her. There was obviously a great deal of Tiffany to stare at.

Sol Cohen's Kosher Deli was indeed sad to see two of its favorite customers leave.

Even the old time crusty waiters shed a fake tear.

Bobby had been an exceptionally good tipper.

It was not his money.

It was HIS.

ROME WAS NOT BUILT IN A DAY. ACTUALLY IT TOOK A LOT LONGER. I SHOULD KNOW, I WAS THERE.

Few people know it was HE who named it the Eternal City. That had to be way back before that ridiculous rumor that the twin sons of Mars, God of War and Rhea Silvia; Romulas and Remus, were supposedly abandoned by dear old mom and suckled by a she wolf.

NONSENSE. I HAPPENED TO KNOW WHO SUCKLED THEM. I'M JUST NOT TALKING. I MADE A PROMISE AND YOU KNOW HOW THAT GOES.

No one was listening at the moment, but HE felt better. HE hated unfounded rumors.

HE was pleased with the progress of the Ambassadors of Love. It would take time but all the projections were good. It would be a good fifteen to twenty five years, depending on what part of the world he was tracking, before any significant results would be seen.

Charts and wall projections were set up in the Peace Room. Updates would be posted quarterly. It would be pretty much of a flat line for the first few years.

Progress takes time.

Rome was something HE could not get out of his craw. It was so carefully planned. HE thought back to the eighth century, the very beginning. The new master plan, where the Papacy was the ruler of the city. The details took years and years to come to fruition. And look what happened in the end. The very birthplace of Western Civilization had gone to hell in a handbag, to use a non godly expression. And why?

Debauchery. Lust. Greed, Self indulgence.

As Claude Rains, as Captain Renault in *Casablanca* once said, 'All the usual suspects'.

THE ETERNAL SHTUP

It was unforgivable.

IT WILL NOT HAPPEN AGAIN. THIS IS MY UNIVERSE. LET OTHER UNIVERSES DO WHAT THEY WANT, BUT HERE, I AM STILL THE BIG CHEESE.

It took a few minutes but HE got it out of his system. He was ready to send Morris and Veronica on another mission, sort of what they do at Brigham Young University. At BYU the kids came back with a whole new prospective and were far better off for the experience. Far better than a week in Lauderdale for Spring Break.

WE ALL KNOW WHERE THAT LEADS. NOT ON MY WATCH.

It seemed Veronica and Morris were having some problems. Maybe too strong a word. They had different points of view on the sustained use of esoteric love. For Morris the novelty was wearing off quickly. It was a good idea but like steak and eggs every morning for breakfast, at times cereal and milk or coffee and a Danish just seemed right.

More natural. More comfortable. More satisfying. Sort of like snap, crackle and pop.

Veronica definately liked the no contact orgasm. Not only was it unique and took a measure of mind control, it was far easier on the body. There were never yeast infections or soreness the morning after. Morris made it clear, the old way, the way it had been done since, well since Adam and Eve, was his first choice for ultimate satisfaction.

HE listened with renewed interest. HE began to think; to wonder; even to question.

I AM THE CREATOR OF EVERYTHING IN THE UNIVERSE AND YET I HAVE NEVER CREATED ANYTHING MYSELF. I HAVE ALLOWED OTHERS TO ACTUALLY CREATE LIFE. I HAVE NEVER HAD A WIFE, A LOVER, A MATE. I HAVE NEVER EXPERIENCED WHAT IT IS LIKE TO HAVE PHYSICAL CONTACT WITH A WOMAN.

HE sat alone on a mini cloud in Section C, like the great French sculpture, Rodin's Thinker, with his head resting in the palm of his hand. HE wanted to be alone. HE needed to be alone.

DID I MAKE A MISTAKE? HOW CAN I INSTRUCT OTHERS IN WHAT I HAVE NEVER EXPERIENCED MYSELF. IT IS LIKE THE PRIESTS WHO TEACH COUPLES ON MARRIAGE PROBLEMS. WHAT DO THEY KNOW? HOW CAN THEY PREACH WHAT THEY HAD NO ACTUAL KNOWLEDGE OF?

As to actual experiences, HE was thinking of boy/girl relationships, not boy/boy.

HE was now in a quandary.

HOW WOULD I PICK A MATE? WHAT QUALIFICATIONS WOULD SHE NEED TO HAVE? HOW WOULD OTHERS PERCEIVE ME? WHY WOULD I EVEN CARE? WOULD IT MAKE ME A MORE UNDERSTANDING, A MORE COMPASSIONATE, A MORE FORGIVING GOD? IS IT NOW TOO LATE?

THE ETERNAL SHTUP

HE thought about some of the women now residing in HIS kingdom. Helen of Troy, Katherine the Great, the original Queen Elizabeth, Cleopatra, Madam Currie, Elizabeth Taylor, Bridget Bardot, Marlene Dietrich, Eleanor Roosevelt. Maybe not Eleanor. She was one great lady, but not so much in the looks department.

I ALMOST FORGOT RITA HAYWARD AND GRETA GARBO. BOTH GREAT LOOKERS WITH TO DIE FOR, BODIES.

The Greats, the near Greats and all the wannabees greats.

The list was obviously endless.

WOULD IT BE FOR COMANIONIONSHIP, TO MATE WITH, TO BE MY BFF? WHAT?

HE was getting a king size headache. Too many what ifs and no real answers. HE knew the matter could not be summarily dismissed. HE had the finest minds in the entire universe at his beck and call. Why not take advantage of it?

I WILL. I WILL.

19

"DO I NEED A MATE? SHOULD I HAVE A WIFE?"

This was a first. They all sat around on a big puffy old cloud and pondered the question, clearly one they had not anticipated or even knew where to begin. HE was the creator. It was HIS kingdom. HE could do whatever he wanted. The question of need or should, had never been brought up before. No one knew where to begin.

It was Tommy Jefferson, definitely not a philosopher who came up with an idea, an interesting thought.

"Shouldn't the people decide? Not a bunch of worldly scholars."

Jeff was big on the "of the people, by the people and for the people" concept.

It got him to where he is today. Or at least to where he was until the fourth of July, how appropriate, 1826. The cause of death was listed as a severe case of diarrhea.

THE ETERNAL SHTUP

BULL SH-T. IT WAS ACTUALLY COLON CANCER. THEY JUST DIDN'T KNOW IT AT THE TIME.

Tommy was interrupted by a familiar voice in the crowd with a distinct foreign accent.

"They are not qualified. Let them decide one issue and next thing you know, they will want a voice in everything," came the sharp response from Leo Tolstoy.

The heavily weighted supersize cloud was now overrun with know-it-alls. There were the politicians, the philosophers, the scientists and those who liked to hear the sound of their own voices. It quickly became chaos.

"ENOUGH, ENOUGH ALREADY."

It took a few seconds for all those present to realize who had just spoken. The room became deathly; better make that, Godly quiet.

"I THINK I NEED TO SLEEP ON IT. THANK YOU ALL FOR YOUR INPUT."

The cloud was immediately empty.

HE had opened a can of worms and everyone knew it.

If HE had a mate, a BFF, he could discuss all sorts of problems with her. But the question remained, did he want a best friend forever and if so, who. HE needed a mate to help him decide if he wanted a mate.

It was a typical *Catch 22* situation.

Veronica and Morris did not have that particular problem. HE had been a good matchmaker. There was no question HE arranged the meeting. With the millions and millions of choices they both had, the odds of them coincidentally meeting were greater than Napoleon stumbling upon Josephine, John Lennon finding Yoko Ono or Marilyn marrying both Joe DiMaggio and Arthur Miller.

MAYBE OPPOSITES DO ATTRACT.

Things like that just don't happen, they are ordained. They are preordained.

No question about it, the meeting of Morris and Veronica was arranged, by HIM.

Thank G-D, Morris thought.

"YOU'RE WELCOME. NOW IT'S MY TURN."

The decision had been made, by the only one who could or should make it.

HIM.

"LET THE TRUMPETS SOUND, FROM THIS DAY, LET THE WORD GO FORTH, LET THE SEARCH BEGIN."

THE ETERNAL SHTUP

The kingdom was immediately in turmoil. Sorta like a giant reality show but this was real. Honest to HIM. The ladies, all the ladies, were in a tizzy. The odds-makers would have a field day. Would HE 'court' his intended? Would HE play the field? Would HE conduct interviews or would he simply announce his choice? HE had never dated. As far as anyone knew, HE had never had an intimate, better make that sexual, relationship with anyone. HE was a loving God but what he was talking about was a whole other thing.

Speculation ran rampant. Like a herd of wild horses on the pampas.

The Ambassadors of Love. With all the guessing and thinking and evaluating, HE had not checked up on Kumbasa and that sensuous looking lady of his, Ubangee in some time. HE had not used the term 'sensuous looking lady' in years, decades, maybe centuries. Who knows how long? Was there a new appreciation; a new mind set in HIS thinking?

Apparently so.

Tiffany swore HE had been watching her in a very non-fatherly way. She was positive he was looking right through her robe or toga or whatever she was wearing. At one point she thought she saw him smile and wink at her. On another occasion, as she was walking away she could feel HIS eyes boring in on her backside.

HE knew she wore no panties and her ass could only be described by all who had the pleasure of indulging, as round, firm and tightly packed. Like a pack of Lucky Strike cigarettes. She did not have the nerve to turn around and look to make sure. Tiff casually held her hands together, behind her back, as she walked away.

She could almost sense HIS disappointment.

There are a hundred, a thousand, ten thousand great bodies up here, go hit on someone else, Tiffany thought.

THANKS, BUT I HAPPEN TO LIKE YOURS.

Tiffany had a horrible thought. She tried to keep it to herself. Was it possible HE was horny and she was the object of his affection?

WOULD THAT REALLY BE SO HORRIBLE TIFF. I'M A NICE GUY ONCE YOU REALLY GET TO KNOW ME. AND YOU WOULD BE SURPRISED AT WHAT I KNOW AND CAN DO.

Tiff suddenly recalled an exclamation she screamed during her last gigantic orgasm.

"O M G"

I TOLD YOU SO.

Tiffany began to run, she was not sure where. Her face was a bright red. She had never been so embarrassed in her whole life, or even afterwards.

THE ETERNAL SHTUP

'THIS IS HEAVEN TIFFANY, NOWHERE TO RUN; NOWHERE TO HIDE."

She still kept running.

OMG, what do I do now?

"STOP RUNNING. COME BACK AND TALK TO ME."

Tiff slowed down to a walk. She was afraid to look back. The problem was, HE was everywhere.

MY KINGDOM. MY RULES, HE was heard to mutter.

Kumbasa and Ubangee were still in Eastern Africa. They had spent time in the Ivory Coast, Ghana and Liberia. It was now time to report back home. Cooperation had been far better than expected. Life expectancy was not. First there was the old slave trade. Every fit male, age ten to forty had been fair game. Any healthy female of child bearing age knew it was only a question of when and where. Families were torn and human rights were something read about in books.

We need divine intervention, was the cry from one and all.

It took more than one hundred years before there was some semblance of normality or justice. Just when the black man felt safe in his own skin, along came AIDS. No one was safe. The carrier monkeys were everywhere. No one could count the lives lost. It took years to get it under control.

Next there was Ebola.

Why does HE hate the black man so much? What have we done to offend HIM? What can we do to get back in HIS trust, HIS good graces?

All good questions.

Kumbasa and Ubangee had the answer, well at least part of the answer. By this time the good citizens were willing to try anything. As everyone knows, timing is everything. Being in the right place at the right time was the key to success. They were there to help.

The natives ate it up like a bowl of just right porridge.

As long as it pleased HIM.

The birth rate dropped to practically zero. The men were too scared to do anything and the women wouldn't let them try on a bet.

All Kumbasa knew was results counted. How they were achieved was another matter.

It was now time to come home.

20

Tiffany would merely serve as a well respected and highly ambitious teacher. No more. There was not a chance in, well let's just say there was never a chance Tiffany would end up as HIS wife. Or mate. Or BFF. She was there to teach. Period.

She was not pleased. She was being used and both HE and she knew it. Soon everyone would know it. Tiffany was going to do what Satin had thought about for a million years.

She was told she had the option of saying no.

Sure. Right. Swell.

Sorry oh Holiest Emperor of the Universe, it's alright for me to bang every Tom, Dick and Harry at the golf range, but just not you. Go down to earth and convince all those lost souls I was doing YOUR work and show them how to jack off by themselves. I have no problem in spreading my legs for half the poor souls up here, but when YOU want a little, just to practice, so you will look like you know what you're doing with YOUR new girlfriend or whenever, the vault is suddenly open. But that's the only time. My guess is I will soon become persona non grata. Thanks, but no thanks.

Tiffany was always a fast learner. It got her where she was today.

"I would be honored and pleased to help you with whatever you want to learn, SIR."

Tiffany was afraid to even think it.

So now I'm HIS bitch.

And she was.

HE decided now was a good time to practice the old adage, *Silence is golden.*

HE did not respond.

As the old joke goes, when an out-of-towner asked a typical New Yorker how to get to Carnegie Hall, the cynical local replied, "Practice, practice, practice."

HE had no intention of ever going to one of the most prestigious classical music venues in the world to practice. The fact was, HE had never visited the Hall located two blocks from Central Park between 56th and 57th on Seventh Avenue. The less people who knew what he had in mind, definitely the better. HE, the creator of man and a few days later woman, had no actual working, hands on knowledge of how all the parts interacted. Sure he had seen man copulate for thousands and thousands of years. HE knew what went where and obviously why. But he never experienced the actual pleasure of doing IT. There is a big difference between reading a recipe on how to make a Devil's food cake and actually kneading the dough, getting your fingers in it, sticking it in the oven and watching it rise to perfection.

Of course, the proof was always in the tasting.

Tiffany was now wearing a full wrap-around apron, and nothing else.

HE was impressed. Nervous, frustrated, anxious maybe a bit embarrassed but definitely impressed. After a few preliminary sessions HE was clearly beginning to get the hang of it.

No pun intended.

Tiffany, bless her soul, and yes HE did, was feeling a bit more relaxed. This was far from her normal gig. Normally her role was not to please him; she was never a professional, but to have a good time. If it was good for her, good for him, it was a good day for all. This was different. She was not sure how far to push the envelope, or anything else. She was not sure what was acceptable behavior and what was off limits.

Does he want to learn just the basics or the whole enchilada, she wondered?

"EVERYTHING. LEAVE NOTHING OUT. I WANT TO BE ALL IN."

They both had to laugh at his double entendre.

It finally hit Tiff like a ton of bricks.

O M G, I'm shtupping HIM.

'YES YOU ARE TIFF, YES YOU ARE - AND PLEASE DON'T STOP ON MY ACCOUNT. I'M REALLY ENJOYING YOUR INSTRUCTIONS."

"Your wish is my command."

"YOU BET YOUR ASS IT IS. THANKS."

Tiff redoubled her efforts.

After what seemed like hours later, the two of them lay on a soft cloud, sort of like a roll of Charmin. They were exhausted. It had been a novel experience – for both of them.

"SAME TIME TOMMORROW TIFF?"

"Same time tomorrow Sir. Have a nice day."

It felt strange calling him Sir, especially after what they had just done. After all, HE was not a John. And she was damn sure not getting paid. At least not in the traditional sense.

HE was in remarkably good spirits, almost giddy. If one did not know better, you would have thought HE had just gotten, well had a satisfying, almost a religious experience. And you would have been right.

Tiff cancelled all lessons, golf or otherwise for the rest of the day, for the rest of the week, actually she was now booked solid with one person. She was on a mission. HE wanted a cram course, sort of like a BA, MA and PhD in a matter of weeks. The only question was, was HE up to it?

"YES I AM. YES I AM."

Tiffany took a nap.

A much needed and well earned nap.

She was asleep the moment her head hit the pillow. HE was still a bundle of energy.

21

It was not a question of pass/fail or whether HE deserved an A or not. It was as natural a thing as Man and God could possibly be. No, it was more about technique, style, individuality, that they were working towards. Tiffany was not surprised; HE was a fast learner, a quick study, a highly motivated student.

HE had no idea who the recipient of all this knowledge would be.

First things first.

Veronica was one of the first to notice the change. It was as if Tiffany had a glow about her. She seemed to be constantly preoccupied. Her ever present smile was dazzling; her skin looked as soft as a baby's ass, her hair literally shined. It looked like she had spent the last week in an executive spa. She was now actually walking on clouds. HIS clouds.

OMG, Tiff's in love.

THE ETERNAL SHTUP

YES SHE IS.

Veronica was not the only one to spot the difference. If she was in love, everyone knew with whom. Everyone loves God, but to be in love with HIM was far, far different.

HE clearly knew it and had to find a way to let her know, without crushing her feeling, and losing one of the best teachers in the universe, that it was mere infatuation on her part. Everyone loves HIM. This time it was not emotional or spiritual. To Tiff it was purely physical. This had never happened before. There was no precedent. HE had never allowed it to happen in the past million years.

WHAT DO I DO NOW?

No one in their right mind was about to give HIM advice. Not if they wanted to remain in HIS kingdom.

Tiff was right on time for their next lesson. In fact she was fifteen minutes early. She had on a new toga that had been tailored to bring out her best features, though that was obviously not necessary.

"TIFF, WE NEED TO TALK. PLEASE HAVE A SEAT, STAY DRESSED AND LISTEN TO ME."

'We need to talk' is a universal sign of problems. Tiff knew that. Every woman who was ever in a relationship knew that. Tiffany sat down on a wisp of a cloud and began to pout, not that it ever had done any good in the past. The fact was, it

was usually she that made that ominous statement to past friends and lovers.

"TIFF, I THOUGHT I MADE IT CLEAR FROM THE BEGINNING. I WAS LOOKING FOR A STUDENT / TEACHER RELATIONSHIP AND FELT YOU WERE THE BEST. IN FACT YOU ARE. BUT I NEVER MADE YOU ANY PROMISES. I NEVER INDICATED THIS WOULD BECOME A ROMANTIC RELATIONSHIP. THE FACT IS, I AM NOT SURE IF I CAN EVER ENTER INTO A ROMANTIC / PHYSICAL RELATIONSHIP. IT WOULD HURT TOO MANY PEOPLE. IF YOU WANT TO STOP THE LESSONS RIGHT NOW, I TOTALLY UNDERSTAND."

She said nothing though there were tears streaming down her cheeks. She slowly, very slowly, sensually removed her new toga, stood to her full height, stretched her body to full length and spread her arms wide in a welcoming gesture. She was flawless, truly magnificent.

She waited so HE could take it all in.

"Are YOU here to talk or to shtup? There is still a great deal for you to learn. Shall we get started?"

Tiffany had taken a liking to the new word in her vocabulary. It was naughty yet not vulgar; it was highly suggestive yet warmly protective. It felt like strawberry flavored KY gel as it slid out over her tantalizing tongue.

HE took one long look at what was being offered to him and breathed heavily.

THE ETERNAL SHTUP

Even HE could not resist.

Tiff had heard HIM loud and clear. She was the teacher, HE was the student. She took this to be a mandate. She had no intention of babying HIM or allowing him a break. She was there to teach and she intended to do just that.

"No, no, no. It's not a football or a baseball bat. It's warm and alive and sensitive and must be approached with all the TLC you have. Now, let's try it again, from the top."

HE looked frustrated. No one had ever spoken to him like that before. Ever.

"Practice damn it, practice. One more time. And this time with feeling. Like you really mean it."

HE was ready to tell her the lesson was over. Permanently.

NO ONE TALKS TO ME WITH THAT TONE OF VOICE. NO ONE. DOES SHE KNOW WHO SHE IS TALKING TO?

"Are YOU here to learn or just stand there and play with yourself?"

Tiff held her breath. She knew what she said had boarded on blasphemy. No, it was blasphemy.

The silence was deafening. The room had turned to ice. HE was trying to decide whether to let it go or not.

Neither spoke for several seconds.

She was hurting but what she said was indefensible.

"I'm so, so sorry. Please forgive me."

HE was still contemplating what he should do. Then he looked at her nude body one more time. Lennie could not have painted a better picture. HE would never know if it was lust or compassion, nor at that moment did he care, that motivated him.

"ALRIGHT. LET'S GET ON WITH IT."

Tiffany smiled and her body radiated warmth and love and passion. She knew this would probably be the last time she would ever make love to HIM. She threw herself into it with such gusto, such force, such determination, such emotion, that HE was afraid she would permanently injure herself.

HE tried his best to keep up with her.

Honest.

When they were finally finished, neither said a word. They were spent. They were both covered with oils and sweet smells and sweat. They were totally exhausted. There was nothing left to say.

They lay on the soft cloud and rested.

NOW I UNDERSTAND WHY THEY NEED A CIGARETTE. TO REST. TO REGAIN STRENGTH. TO BUY TIME.

THE ETERNAL SHTUP

Tiffany knew there was no need for any more lessons. There was nothing left for HIM to learn. There was nothing left for her to teach. HE had taken the final exam and passed with flying colors.

HE got HIS A.

An A for effort, an A for endurance and an A for performance.

A thank you by either one of them would have been superfluous.

For the first time in as long as HE could remember, HE closed HIS eyes and took a short nap.

HE had earned it.

Tiff smiled. There was no better compliment than the guy went to sleep.

She had done her job. And had done it well.

YES YOU DID.

22

Word spread like wildfire or the lead story in the *National Enquirer*. HE had had a fling with Tiffany and it ended quickly and very badly. As the story circulated, it picked up momentum of its own. Like every rumor, the more one denied, the more the masses believed.

It was a no win situation.

Tiffany decided to quit her day job and spend more time on a few far-away clouds in Section B.

HE had no such option.

HE was there to rule. And rule he did. HE also had two other matters on HIS mind. One was the Ambassadors of Love and the second; did he want and need a wife/companion/mate? The second was obviously the most troubling.

HE truly had no idea where or how to begin.

THE ETERNAL SHTUP

Veronica wanted to give HIM some advice, but it was certainly not her place.

What would she say?

"Sir; waking up in the morning alone is the pits. Not having anyone to snuggle with all night is downright frightening. Trying to talk to yourself when there is a problem is absolutely frustrating."

Then she came up with the best possible reason ever. HE did it himself. HE knew Adam needed a mate. HE understood all the reasons, rationale and ramifications. It was HIS idea that Man should not live alone. Man needs a mate. HIS own words, or close to it. How could he argue with his own logic?

As always, HE was listening. And HE agreed, Veronica was right.

TO ARGUE AGAINST HER IS TO ARGUE AGAINST MYSELF.

For the second time in a very few days, HE again knew what he had to do.

Now that HE knew what HE needed, HE needed to know who. Certainly someone UP HERE. Someone he had met before. Someone who would feel the same way he thought and felt.

But who?

THE LIST IS ENDLESS. WHERE DO I BEGIN? AT THE BEGINNING OF COURSE.

HE thought about all the great sirens of the last few thousand or so years. HIS first thought was perhaps a long walk; there were no Starbucks or coffee houses to hang out in with Helen of Troy. Word had it; she was the most beautiful woman of the world, at the time. Her father, Zeus, King of the Gods, attested to her good stock. Her mother Leda was no charwoman either. Her abduction, whether real or conceived by her to bring about more attention to herself, brought about the Trojan Wars.

NOT A SMART MOVE, HELEN BABY.

It had been rumored at one time she had many lovers, which bothered HIM, and was now lonely and helpless.

ANYONE THAT CUNNING AND BEAUTIFUL CANNOT POSSSIBLY BE HELPLESS. I WILL HAVE TO APPROACH HER WITH THE UTMOST OF CARE.

HE had nothing to lose. HE knew where she was at all times. HE knew where everyone was – at all times. Part of the job description.

"Your Holiness, have I done something wrong?"

"Oh no Helen. I just thought it was about time I got to say hello to you. You've been here for what, two thousand, twenty five hundred years now."

THE ETERNAL SHTUP

Helen blushed and refused to look him in the eye.

"Actually only two thousand four hundred and eighty seven. But who's counting."

SHE SEEMS DOWNRIGHT SKIDISH. DROP DEAD GEORGOUS WITH THOSE RAVEN CURLS DOWN TO HER NECK, BUT APPEARS TO BE AFRAID OF HER OWN SHADOW.

"SO TELL ME HELEN, WHAT DO YOU DO TO HAVE FUN UP HERE. WHO DO YOU HANG WITH? YOU WERE ALWAYS POPULAR WITH THE YOUNG MEN WHEN YOU WERE ALIVE, ALL THOSE BATTLES AND LIVES LOST YOU KNOW. WERE YOU ABDUCTED OR DID YOU REALLY ELOPE?"

Now her face was beet red. She began to hyperventilate and clutched her ample bosom. She was on the verge of tears. HE wondered how she would act if William Jennings Bryant were cross examining her.

NOT A CHANCE IN HADES.

"Sir, those are dirty rotten rumors. I swear to you. I didn't start any war. And I'll have you know I was a virgin till the day I became married. Now if you will excuse me Sir, I have some friends to meet."

HE knew she was lying. Both about the abduction, the virginity thing and having to meet some friends. He also knew she was a daddy's girl. All she had to do was put her head down and whine and Zeus would come through. Definitely not what HE was looking for. The last thing he needed was a hookup with a habitual liar.

"HAVE FUN AND BE SURE TO SAY HELLO TO ALL YOUR FRIENDS FOR ME. BYE."

It would be another twenty five hundred years before HE would talk to her again.

SO, BACK TO SQUARE ONE.

Little things like God tiptoeing through the tulips with a charming if totally dishonest young lady, did not go unnoticed. Everyone wanted to fix HIM up. The question was with whom and who would be the lucky matchmaker?

When word got to Tiffany who had recently moved to the very tip of Cloud Ten, she sat right down and cried. Big salty tears that did not seem to end.

Morris and Veronica were off on another official visit to Mother Earth. This time to Great Britain. The Muslims living there were populating the East End of London like little jack rabbits on uppers. Morris had no idea in the world how to approach them.

MAYBE WE'LL HAVE TO USE SOMETHING OUT OF THIS WORLD.

Few people would have ever dreamed UP HERE was pretty much Open Enrollment. St. Peter did NOT stand at the gate

THE ETERNAL SHTUP

like a TSA security guard going through your baggage and asking all sort of embarrassing questions. It was now facial recognition and chips. Sure Michael Mason was persona non grata. Hitler, Idi Amin from Uganda and all mass murderers were sent directly to Hell, but tax evaders, cheating wives and most lawyers were summarily forgiven.

HE did not have the time to waste on petty matters.

The big surprise to most new arrivals was the presence of Moses, Buddha, Confucius, Jesus Christ and all the great religious leaders of the past two to five thousand years. Why not? All were welcome. The unwritten rule was respect. No one had to agree with what they were saying but at least give them the opportunity, in an open forum, to be heard. Arguing, if handled appropriately, was not only accepted, it was expected. And encouraged. Verbal was permitted; physical was forbidden.

MLK could attest to that first hand. Rev. King, known to one and all as Marty K believed in two things. One was the process of non violence. In the long run, more could be accomplished by peaceful demonstrations. That did not always feel right to one whose head, arms and legs had come into contact multiple times with a leaded Billy club. The good old boys in the Deep South felt by putting on a blue cop suit and wearing a badge, It gave them the right to crack open as many black heads, knees and arms as their strength allowed.

And what was Martin Luther King's other belief? Not a particularly well kept secret. Finding a young, innocent black girl, taking her behind the barn or in the back room of his church and shoving the fear of the Lord into her.

As often as he could.

It was his most private way of allowing them to be at one with thy Maker.

Marty was now invited to the table whenever there was a big pow wow. He tried to sit next to one of the Kennedys or a powerful white man who had been there for centuries.

It was good for his image.

HE was too busy to worry about image. Who was there to question it?

NOBODY. THERE BETTER BE NOBODY.

Cleopatra was already on HIS short list. None could deny her beauty, wit and charm, not to mention her liaison with Julius Caesar and upon his assassination, quickly marrying Mark Antony. Cleo always represented herself as the reincarnation of an Egyptian goddess.

CLOSE, BUT NO CIGAR.

Being Queen of Egypt was one thing. Being the wife of HIM was a whole other ball of wax. And then some. She was sure she was right for the job and right for HIM.

THE ETERNAL SHTUP

She made no bones about it.

There was no Nile to take strolls along. There were no gourmet kitchens to show HIM how creative she was. There was only her body and her smile. On a few occasions HE had politely mentioned the scoop line of her toga was a bit too risqué. HE knew exactly what she had. There was no need to advertise it.

THIS IS NOT GOING AS I PLANNED.

It was not as if HE was eavesdropping. Everyone knew HE knew what they were thinking.

It was not as if HE was a prude and it was sure not from a lack of knowhow but when Cleo suggested they take the next step, **THERE'S ONLY ONE STEP LEFT**, HE tactfully put on the brakes.

TOO MUCH, TOO SOON. WHY THE BIG HURRY?

They were going nowhere soon. There are many ways to seal a deal. This was not the one HE had in mind. Without totally closing the door, HE suggested perhaps they cool their jets for a few days. Sort of see how things played out.

No one has ever refused my favors before. I just offered HIM what men have fought and actually died for, and HE said thanks but no thanks, Cleopatra thought.

THERE'S ALWAYS A FIRST FOR EVERYTHING MY DEAR.

At that moment HE made up his mind. The only question was how to tell her? She was not used to NO. When she realized it was not going to be an exclusive relationship, she would understand. It was not as if her favors were not sought by a good five thousand men already. Her dance card had been filled for years and years.

Before getting back to HIS short list, there were other matters to look at. Then HE had one last thought on this dating thing.

WHY SHOULD I LIMIT MYSELF TO THE SHORT LIST? I CAN PICK ANYONE, EVEN MOLLY O'BRIEN, WHO I HAVE HAD MY EYE ON FOR WHAT, A COUPLE OF HUNDRED YEARS?

23

Molly Margret O'Brien had been somewhat of a legend in her native Ireland. Feisty was not strong enough a word for her contempt for the movement against her own people. She organized rallies, made great pots of food to feed those who needed nourishment and did everything to make herself a giant pain in the ass to those who disagreed with her. She was a large, yet well proportioned woman with an enormous heart, a bushel basket of love and a massive appetite for giving. She was a mere thirty one years old, had never been married and never born children when she was struck and killed by a runaway horse more than two hundred twenty two years ago.

Her hair was red and fell to below her shoulders. Her eyes were blue and clear of fright. She took no guff from any man, regardless of wealth, fame or fortune.

Molly was truly an original.

HE liked that.

She was also a Catholic.

HE liked that also.

HE was quick to point out religion was not important UP HERE. It was who you were not what you were. HERE was a hodgepodge of religions, cultures and ethnic backgrounds.

Molly was of peasant stock and proud as hell, forgive the expression, of it. Her education was limited to grade school but over the past two hundred years she read everything. The good, the bad and the ugly. If you did not like her, well that was your problem. Not hers. Molly had an opinion on everything and made no bones about telling you exactly what she thought.

Molly was more than mildly surprised when HE appeared as she was leaving the library. It was not a coincidence, this she was sure of. To the best of her knowledge she had not used HIS name in vain in some time. She had been close but had not crossed the line in her opinions on several recent political matters, especially those involving Catholics and Protestants.

"MAY I INTEREST YOU IN A WALK SO WE CAN GET TO KNOW EACH OTHER BETTER?"

"Of course. There's not much I don't know about you and as for me self, I think I might be a bit boring to you, seeing as how you have all these important people here. But if it's a walking you want, let's be at it."

THE ETERNAL SHTUP

Molly offered her arm and HE accepted.

For an uneducated woman, there was not much that Molly Margret O'Brien was not knowledgeable about.

They walked and talked, talked and walked. I guess you could say she did most of the talking. HE was known far and wide, as a good listener.

There were no parks or avenues, no street signs or benches or rest areas. After what seemed like hours and hours they were back at the library steps. HE was more than impressed. So impressed HE invited her to a violin concerto the following evening. Bach was conducting his own piece. Niccolo Paganini, who was alleged to have sold his soul to the devil, would be playing his 1743 Guarnen. His favorite. It would have been a sellout, STO, but there was always extra cloud space available.

Molly Margret gracefully accepted. She was thrilled. It was her first date in more than fifty years. Actually it was closer to seventy five.

They had front cloud seats.

There was something plain and simple and honest about Molly Margret. HE admired that. HE knew he could just be himself, whatever that meant. At times being who HE was, was overwhelming. HE thought it might be fun to disguise himself for a few days and just wonder around and be another nobody. Actually everyone UP HERE was a somebody.

People began to talk. What else did they have to do? There were no cell phones or text messaging or video games to keep busy for hours at a time. There were also no sales at the mall or on cyber space. There were no TV's and no reruns of I Love Lucy. Or MASH, for those who liked that sort of comedy.

Alan Alda had not arrived at the Pearly Gates – yet. HE was looking forward to talking to him. HE wanted to know more about Corporal Klinger.

WAS IT ONE BIG ACT, OR WHAT?

The talk now was all about HIM and Ms. Molly Margret O'Brien. Some good; some not so good. Opinions were like parents, everyone had at least two. At times they only acknowledged one. HE was above it all. It was not the first time HE would be the subject of controversy, far from it. All great wars were begun in HIS name.

Then the original concept somehow got lost.

Molly was beginning to feel self conscious. She felt like she was the side show, the second banana, the tag line to a good joke. She knew she could never compete but at least she wanted, she needed to be taken serious. She felt women were equal at least one hundred and fifty years before the theory became popular. Perhaps she would have a talk with Carrie Nation or Suzy Anthony before moving forward.

Both women made similar comments. Trust, but verify. They had both been burned more than once. Men have different agenda than woman. Nothing complicated about that. It was not as if HE would lie or deceive, HE was who HE was but old habits were difficult to break.

After many a sleepless night Molly decided she liked life as it was. No complications, no changes, no compromises. She decided to send HIM a Dear John letter. It was not actually a written letter but HE got the idea. HE understood.

GUESS ITS BACK TO THE OLD DRAWING BOARD. SHE'S INDEED A FINE LADY, A BIT FIESTY BUT UNSCRUPULOUSLY HONEST.

Bobby was becoming bored. Not with Tiffany, that was one of the best things to ever happen to him, but with the globetrotting assignment to get the good folks to learn greater self control.

The fact was, the better he did his job, the more valuable and indispensible he became. A typical *Catch 22*. If he was doing a lousy job, something he was constitutionally incapable of, he would have been reassigned or fired.

HE was fully aware of the matter.

BE CAREFUL WHAT YOU WISH FOR BOBBY.

HE thought about teaming up Bobby with a new partner, maybe one less experienced and less threatening. RFK was seldom threatened by anyone but if he could take the lead, he would be more enthusiastic. At least that was HIS thinking. HIS first thought was Molly Margret. They had similar backgrounds and could push each other to bring out the best in both of them. The problem was, Molly had never been married, never had children and had no intention of speaking of any such matters from past experiences.

LET ME THINK, WHO ELSE.

Someone suggested Kim Hunter whose claim to fame was playing Stella Kowalski in *Streetcar Named Desire*. She had stage presence, a nice, tight body when she was young and would not upstage Bobby. Kim was known to take chances and would be a good fit for Bobby, no pun intended.

"BOBBY, IF YOU HAVE A MINUTE."

RFK listened.

Kim was a fine actress and knew the ropes but for some reason Bobby did not feel any chemistry. She was good but not right for him. For this new assignment, there had to be something special, someone special. Someone people would listen to.

Bobby had a brain fart. He had to talk to Jack before even suggesting it to HIM. Before Mr. Attorney General could make a move, big brother John was standing next to him.

"You don't need my permission Bobby. If that's what you want, if that's what'll make you happy, go for it."

Jack then messed up Bobby's hair and was gone.

THE ETERNAL SHTUP

Now all Bobby needed was HIS permission, and of course, her OK.

Bobby was sure she would say yes. Especially if Jack and HE gave the okey.

He then approached HIM with his ideas.

"This is what I have in mind, SIR."

Bobby then went on to explain in detail. He did not need to hear it chapter and verse. HE knew what Bobby was thinking before he ever said it.

"Sorry SIR. I guess I wasn't thinking."

HE nodded. No sense in making a Kennedy upset. They had had their share of heartache. Enough for a dozen families. It was like a black cloud constantly following them around.

"AN EXCELLENT IDEA, GOOD CHOICE. DO YOU WANT ME TO ARRANGE IT OR WOULD YOU PREFER TO TALK TO MARILYN FIRST?"

"I think it would be better, more official, if it came from YOU, Sir."

24

"Oh Bobby, I would be honored, I'm thrilled. When can we start?"

Ms. Marilyn Monroe was practically falling out of her toga. Marilyn loved the idea of going braless. She thought bras were a complete waste of time, effort and money. No one really wanted to wear them anyway.

Not unless they were padded.

"Is it OK with Jack?"

She only used his first name in private. At all other times it was Mr. President.

"It has been cleared by everyone, and I do mean Everyone. As to when do we start, there are certain ground rules, the first being, no touching."

"No touching. That can't be right. How can we, you-know, do IT?"

THE ETERNAL SHTUP

"That's the whole idea Marilyn."

"Really? Then why are we doing it at all?"

RFK knew it was now time for a long, long talk. The touching would have to wait for later.

"Have a seat Sweetheart."

Marilyn sat down on a cloud allowing her toga to purposely ride up to her bare thighs. Not only was she bra less, she was also panty less.

HE was watching everything.

"I think I could concentrate better if you crossed your legs dear."

Marilyn smiled. She had been caught. She absentmindedly reached down to pick up a piece of cloud and inadvertently her entire left breast fell out of its temporary prison.

"Sorry Bobby. It's not as if you have not seen them before. Would you like a sample now?"

"I think I can wait. I think we both should wait. Now, let me explain exactly what Esoteric Lovemaking is all about."

"They miss you. Terribly Bobby. Please."

She looked down at her now heaving bosom.

"Enough Marilyn, enough! We are here to learn our lines. To rehearse. Nothing else. Yet. If you learn them quickly, I promise you there will be a reward."

"So where do I start?"

First and foremost, she was an actress.

HE was pleased. Bobby had given her the right motivation.

WHERE SHOULD I SEND THEM? WHERE WILL THEY DO THE MOST GOOD?

The rehearsals had gone well. Better than expected. Marilyn had learned her lines and was the most persuasive of all the ambassadors. It had to be a place where pregnancy ran rampant and both of them were well known. Hollywood was the most obvious but HE felt it was not right.

HARLEM.

The rate of teenage pregnancies was off the charts. The Kennedys always felt welcome above 125th Street in the City and the black girls always looked up to white actresses. Who better than the one and only Marilyn Monroe. The girls could lust for Bobby and the boys would fantasize about her. It was the perfect choice, the perfect location, even if HE had to say so himself.

"Harlem?"

THE ETERNAL SHTUP

"That's what HE said. I don't think arguing will do much good."

"You'll be with me at all times Bobby, to protect me, won't you?"

"Twenty four / Seven, Sugar."

Marilyn felt better. Much better.

"I better start to pack."

"Marilyn, there is no need to bring clothes. What you are wearing is just fine. We will be traveling light. You might want to put a safety pin to cover up some of that cleavage. The boys will be there to hear what you say, not look down your toga to see those succulent titties and rock hard nipples."

The last few words were a mistake. A big mistake. Maybe not really meant as a mistake. Bobby was no dummy. In fact he had calculated on a response.

It completely turned her on and she was not about to take no for an answer.

"Now. And don't you dare say no. It's your fault for exciting me and you damn well know it."

A gentleman never refuses the request of a lady.

Especially under those demanding circumstances.

HE sat, watched, as was HIS right, and smiled.

THEY DO MAKE A REALLY GREAT COUPLE.

The first lecture, though it was not really a lecture, some would describe it as show and tell, was scheduled for the world famous Apollo Theater on 125th. When they announced who would be speaking, tickets were scalped at close to six hundred each.

The actual admission price was free.

Bobby was the first to speak. When it became apparent no one was looking or listening to him, he took his cue and introduced the totally delicious Ms. Boom Boom. Everyone perked up. The boys were mesmerized. They had trouble maintaining eye level contact.

Then the group was divided into boys and girls (really men and women) for a demo. Each group was invited to participate. It became obvious there would have to be several sessions for each group. Each group could not wait to begin.

The results could only be described as – disappointing. There had to be fifty horny black men in a room listening to erotic talk from one of the sexiest women on earth. That in and of itself made no sense. Norma Jean had been dead since 1962 and here she was, in the flesh, so to speak.

"Look, talk, but do not touch."

THE ETERNAL SHTUP

That could almost be considered cruel and inhuman treatment of your genitals.

The boys were not into it, no matter how much Marilyn coaxed.

They tried; you had to give them that. They were all about to quit when one of the boys looked at the expression on Marilyn's face and screamed, "We did it."

Her face turned bright red as she stifled a low groan. Her veins were about to pop out of her neck. Her thighs were pressed tight against each other and were quivering. No question, Marilyn just had an orgasm. The crowd went crazy.

"WE DID IT. WE DID IT. WE DID IT."

Bobby, who was in the next room heard the loud noise and thought the worst. He rushed in to see what was going on. As he entered the room his eyes caught Marilyn's and they locked for a split second. It was only then he knew. He was absolutely positive.

There was a good reason Marilyn was considered a great actor. She had learned what was expected of her and performed eloquently and on cue. She was now on stage, her true home. No one ever knew, on that day, and that day only, she had faked it. It was her role and she played it to perfection.

Bobby stared at her and mouthed the words, *Academy Award.*

Marilyn hid the smile as best as she could. She was still on stage and had to carry it out to the fullest.

The crowd was hooked.

The word spread. The next night and every night for the next ten days, there was not a seat to be had at the Apollo. The boys had learned and learned well. They had made Marilyn do what was considered almost impossible before then. They had used esoteric love – no touching - to make her have a self induced orgasm.

HE was thrilled. Marilyn had them eating out of her hands, to use a figure of speech.

I MUST REMIND MYSELF TO ASK HER TO BE IN OUR NEXT CHRISTMAS PAGENT.

Bobby was also thrilled. He did not mind taking a back seat to Marilyn. Not only did he convince the ladies that it actually worked, but he knew after each performance, Marilyn was still horny as hell from all the suggestive talking and could not wait to give her all – to Bobby.

He was definitely a most happy fella.

GOOD CHOICE. IF I DO SAY SO MYSELF.

25

It seemed like the steps of the library was yesterday's version of a soap box or today's twitter. If you wanted to get something off your chest, that was the place to do it.

Today it was Cleopatra VII Philopator, last active ruler of Ptolemaic, better known simply as Cleopatra, who was letting those who had the time and interest know that Mark Antony, who she was married to for less than a dozen years, was a first class shit. Not only did she have five kids that he fathered, but died at thirty nine years of age.

On August 14, 30 B C

DOESN'T SHE EVER CALL IT QUITS. IT BEEN ALMOST TWENTY ONE HUNDRED YEARS AND SHE'S STLL RAGING ON HIM. IF SHE WERE MY WIFE, ME FORBID, I'VE HAVE TOLD HER TO TAKE HER SMALL PIECE OF MY KINGDOM AND SHOVE IT.

Most of the listeners were men. They had heard it all before but could not take their eyes off her. As usual, she had on the same white chiffon gown with the satin straps that crossed and separated her bosom. She made sure her little tirades were in the late afternoon with the sun lowering behind her. It gave the image her gown was transparent.

WHICH IT NOW IS.

No one ever accused Cleopatra of being a dummy or not taking advantage of every trick she could think of.

"If it were not for me, he would have been just another Roman general, fighting with Octavian for control of the Roman Empire. At least he was smart enough to know an alliance between Egypt, that I controlled, and Rome, where he had a foot up on Octavian, would make him the most powerful man in the world. The son-of-a-bitch, used me. After five kids, my figure was shot to hell. If anyone saw me naked, without the corset type bra and form fitting undergarments, who would lust after me. Why Lizzy Taylor would never have wanted to portray me at the cinema."

YOU'RE RIGHT ABOUT THAT CLEO BABY. I SHOULD KNOW. I'VE SEEN YOU IN YOUR BIRTHDAY SUIT. TOO MANY TIMES, NOW THAT I THINK ABOUT IT.

Cleo spotted HIM in the background. Like everyone else UP HERE, she had heard the rumors.

What could possibly make more sense? Me, Queen of Egypt, actually former Queen of Egypt, Abdel Fattah al Sisi, is now president of Egypt, and the Ruler of the Entire Universe. Whatever happened to the old days? A president? In my day, there were just Kings and Queens. Oil screwed up everything.

THE ETERNAL SHTUP

NO WAY CLEO. I'VE GOT ENOUGH PROBLEMS. LAST THING I NEED IS A WHINY, COMPLAINING QUEEN. THIS PLACE IS ALREADY RUN OVER WITH QUEENS.

HE was about to quietly walk away when HE, like everyone else, heard her shrill voice.

"Oh SIR, if you have a minute? I'd like to discuss something with you."

Cleopatra sucked in her two thousand year old gut and filled her lungs to more than capacity.

I CAN SEE RIGHT THROUGH YOU CLEO. BOTH LITERALLY AND FIGURATIVELY.

"OF COURSE QUEENIE."

HE knew that designation would clearly piss her off.

Cleopatra gave HIM her most alluring smile as she thought, *That was not necessary, you pompous little prick.*

"I STRONGLY SUGGEST YOU APOLOGIZE CLEOPATRA. NOW. THAT IS OUT AND OUT BLASPHEMY. THIS IS ME YOU'RE REFERRING TO. YOU'RE NO LONGER IN YOUR LITTLE SAND CASTLE KINDGOM ON THE NILE."

Cleopatra said nothing.

"I'M WAITING."

The entire audience on the library steps had now heard the wrath of HIM. No one had the nerve to look at either one of them.

Cleopatra was thoroughly humiliated. She was also furious. Both at herself for thinking such a demeaning thought and being reprimanded in public. This would have been impossible back home. The problem was, she was not back home. Where she was now was her home. Forever.

"Forgive me Your Holiness. I know not what I was thinking. I do, with all sincerity apologize.

I DON'T BELIEVE YOU. NOT FOR ONE SECOND.

"YOU ARE FORGIVEN. JUST DON'T LET IT HAPPEN AGAIN. I'M WATCHING AND LISTENING TO YOU. AS TO WHAT YOU WANTED TO DISCUSS WITH ME, THE ANSWER IS A MOST EMPHATIC, NO."

"Thank you, Your Eminence."

"A HORSE, A HORSE, MY KINGDOM FOR A HORSE.

He was thinking more of a woman, preferably a mate, a partner who did not look or act like a horse or an ass. HE remembered how many now residents had talked about people watching. At shopping malls, outlet malls, specialty malls, airports, in line at the DMV office, food stamp lines, waiting for tickets to see a Rolling Stone concert. You name it. People watching was almost an occupation for some older people. For those who wanted a little more mental stimulation there was court watchers. Those people who sat in the first few rows of a courtroom every day and watched the witnesses lie their asses off for a few bucks or marital freedom.

They figured they knew more than the lawyers.

From what HE saw, they probably did.

WE HAVE NO AIRPORTS, MALLS OR COURTROOMS UP HERE SO MAYBE I'LL JUST SPEND SOME TIME STANDING ON THE CORNER, WATCHING ALL THE GIRLS GO BY. BY GOSH, BY GOLLY, THAT'S EXACTLY WHAT I WILL DO.

The thought of soliciting flashed through HIS mind. No way. No way in hell could anyone charge HIM with anything indecent or immoral. HE was HIM. It was not as if HE were inconspicuous. It was not if HE could wear a costume or put on a disguise. HE was clearly the most recognizable person in the clouds. St. Peter came in a distant second. The old days when Pete spent all day, almost every day at the Gate were long gone. Now they used sensors, bar codes, facial recognition and electronic scanning devises.

Far more accurate not to mention less man hours. Peter felt like he was on an extended holiday.

HE briefly wondered if the neighborhood was going to the dogs.

NOT POSSIBLE. NO WAY IN, IN HEAVEN.

HE stood for hours, for days, maybe for weeks, no one kept time, watching, looking, observing, thinking. Who could be the new Mrs. HIM?

Matters of state were put on hold. It was like gridlock in midtown Manhattan heading to one of the tunnels or bridges on a late Friday afternoon in July when everyone wanted to get out of the city and head for the Hamptons or the Jersey shore.

As to the Ambassadors of Love project, everyone was waiting for further instructions. No one was about to approach HIM. Obviously HE had other things on his mind.

Morris and Veronica decided it made sense to live together. They were not sure of protocol. It was not as if each had a lease or owned their separate condos. It was not like they had furniture or clothes or knickknacks or pots and pans or pictures to hang on the walls. Talk about free spirits, everyone UP HERE was a free spirit.

They were pretty sure HE did not have to be contacted for approval. HE knew what they were doing and probably when and how. HE had more important things to worry about then signing off on conjugal rights and who was living with whom. There seemed to be no shortage of accommodations. One bedroom looked pretty much the same as another.

Veronica wondered at times if they were sleeping in the same bed every night or was it hit and miss. And what about the sheets? Surely they were changed every day.

THE ETERNAL SHTUP

"I don't think it will hurt to talk to HIM. So far we have gotten along famously."

Veronica nodded at Morris. Whatever he wanted was all right with her, as long as he did not upset the apple cart. There were no carts, apple or otherwise, that she could see.

"Excuse me, Sir. I know you're very busy but if you have half a minute to talk to me?"

"A HALF A MINUTE, A FULL MINUTE, A HALF A DAY, ALL DAY. WHAT'S THE DIFFERENCE MORRIS? TIME MEANS NOTHING HERE. TALK TO ME MY LITTLE BROTHER."

"Well it's about Veronica and me."

"IS THERE A PROBLEM? YOU WANT MAYBE YOU SHOULD FIND SOMEONE ELSE. YOU HAVE MY PERMISSION. GO AND BE HAPPY."

"No, no. It's nothing like that Sir. We love each other and want to live together. Like being married but no children and no legal obligations. No alimony if things don't work out. You know, stuff like that. We thought we should run it by YOU first. We're not sure what the rules are here."

"YOU'RE SUCH A GOOD BOY MORRIS. I TRULY APPRECIATE THAT. NO, YOU DO NOT NEED SPEICAL DISPENSATION FROM ME – OR ANYONE. JUST BE HAPPY AND ENJOY. WE BOTH KNOW WHAT YOU ENJOY, DON'T WE?"

"Thank you Sir."

"ANYTIME BOYCHICK."

HE liked to use slang or words of comfort whenever HE could. Morris' father called him Boychick, a term of true endearment, when he was a small boy.

That all changed after the Bar Mitzvah. He was no longer a boy, he was now a man. Morris was now no longer a man; he was a spirit, a spirit of the man he was on earth.

26

Morris was pleased he had HIS blessing. He wanted to go back to his place to tell Veronica when again it came to him. Where was his place? Did he actually have a place? Did he and Veronica have their own place? Did they actually sleep in a bed and was it their own bed. It was all so confusing. And how long would it last? How long would he be with Veronica? Would they ever grow old?

How long is eternity?

Morris was troubled by the concept. He knew he was surrounded by the best minds ever to think. From Abraham, Isaac and Moses, assuming you believed in the Old Testament, to Jesus and the Apostles, to Plato and Aristotle, to Einstein and Steve Jobs.

As to Billy Gates, who was still DOWN THERE, he was at the right place at the right time. From a Harvard classroom to a small garage alongside his parent's home in Redmond, Washington. Who would'a thought it?

I WOULD.

Certainly someone had to know how long eternity was.

Morris wondered if he would ever tire of Veronica and if so, when. It did not immediately occur to him that perhaps Veronica could tire of him.

A TYPICAL MALE ATTITUDE, MORRIS.

HE was listening in, as usual, but felt Morris had to figure some things out for himself. HE said nothing.

The parade of women in front of the library, a place to see and be seen, was incredible. It was like Broadway and 42nd Street, the square in front of the Eiffel Tower and Piccadilly Circus in London all rolled into one. HE thought back to the Coliseum and the Parthenon in the good old days. HE saw movie stars looking like they were in their prime, women of great power in politics, many of the women behind the man. HE felt like a kid in a candy store with a sweet tooth and a pocket full of coin.

So he sat and watched and wondered. And prayed.

WHO IS RIGHT FOR ME? WHO WILL BE MY PARTNER, MY LOVER, MY BEST FRIEND?

For the first time in decades, maybe centuries, probably longer, HE closed his eyes. HE was tired and needed a nap. Without thinking HE put his head down on the cloud. In the twinkle of an eye, HE was fast asleep. No one had ever seen

THE ETERNAL SHTUP

HIM fast asleep before. No one knew HE snored. Loudly. It was a sight no one who witnessed it, would ever forget.

HE dreamed. Boy did HE dream. It was like a casting party with one beautiful woman after another parading past him. He slept, snored and smiled. It was driving everyone crazy. Finally Charlton Heston sauntered up and gave HIM the slightest of nudges. Enough to wake him up. Charlie had mistakenly assumed his roles in the *Ten Commandments* and *Ben Hur* gave him some type of preferred status. Whatever good will he may have garnered as a leader of civil rights in the 60's, went right out the window when he became the spokesman for the NRA.

BIG, BIG MISTAKE, CHARLIE.

Charlton had only been UP HERE for less than seven years and was still a wet-behind-the-ears rookie. HE did not appreciate being woken, especially while talking to the very giddy Dolly Madison and let Charlie know it. He should keep his hands to himself. The fact he may have played Moses, did not in fact make him Moses.

EVEN MOSES WOULD NOT TOUCH ME WITHOUT PERMISSION. NOT WITH A TEN FOOT SHAFT.

Heston apologized and beat a quick retreat. HE asked Peter to make a note that Heston not be included in any further guest lists. The man was a bore and was too into himself. If given half a chance, Charlie would have believed he was HIM.

ACTORS, THEY ARE SO NAÏVE, THEY BEGIN TO BELIVE THEY ARE WHO THEY PLAYED, HA. NOT ON MY WATCH. WHERE WAS I? OH YES, DOLLY MADISON.

Dolly had been hanging around HERE since just before the Civil War, around the late 1840's as HE recalled. Born a Quaker, her first husband, John Payne was a lawyer who died in the plague along with several of their children. She was expelled from the Friends when she married James Madison, definitely not of the faith. Not particularly attractive, she made up for her lack of physical beauty by her social skills. HE found her interesting and communicative, but certainly not partnership material. HE would consider her a friend but not even close to the short list he carried around.

As to The List, it was in constant change. Names were added, names were just as quickly removed. It was almost a game of survival as to who stayed and who didn't. If pari-mutuel betting was allowed, and it wasn't, the bookmakers would have had a field day. A giant board could have been set up just inside the library and the top ten contenders would be listed with the prevailing odds.

The betting would have been merely for sport as there was no money in HIS kingdom. There was no reason for currency. There was nothing to buy. If you wanted something, and it was not owned by another, it was yours. There were no homes or apartments or condos for rent or sale. Everyone knew they had their own personal space to rest their head. No one was quite sure where, however.

THE ETERNAL SHTUP

As to cars or boats or bikes or skateboards, especially skateboards, there were none. There were no car dealerships or gas stations or repair shops or used car lots. There were a number of used car salesmen but many indicated it was only a temporary gig or someone who looked like them, sold the customer the lemon.

DO YOU THINK ANYONE REALLY BELIEVES THAT B.S.

Used car salesmen fell pretty much in the same category as politicians. They did not have to be loved, they did not even have to be believed, but on earth, they were pretty much a necessity.

The same was true for lawyers.

THE PLACE IS LITERALLY CRAWLING WITH THEM.

Honest Abe, Williams Jennings Bryant Justice Earl Warren and Johnny Cochran would have taken exception to that last remark. They took exception to just about everything. That was what they were paid to do. Richard Nixon, an attorney by education, a crook by trade, rightfully pointed out without lawyers there would have been no Magna Charta, no Bill of Rights, no Constitution and no gut wrenching, winner-take-all divorce settlements. And who would there be to chase the ambulances to the hospital emergency entrances?

"Without lawyers, who would write the laws?" Joe McCarthy was once heard to say at a congressional hearing on un-American activities.

"The Commies have lawyers, but they all work for the State. And are controlled by the State."

No one put anything past old Joe.

HE decided to put the partner / mate / companion search on hold for a while. There were far more important matters to concentrate on. There would always be women to find. It was one commodity there was never a shortage of, the tall and the short; the beauties and those who thought they were beauties; those who loved to share and those that wanted to be coaxed. Yes, HE had seen them all. There was time and there was always a variety of product on the well stocked, or was it well stacked, shelves.

HE had not met with Ming Haw Sang and Gintasa or Kumbasa and his long legged beauty Ubangee, in some time. It bothered HIM that every time he thought of Ubangee it was in reference to her long legs. Why with more than a few hundred ex Radio City Rockets strolling around the clouds, long legs should not have been such a big deal. Still, whenever he mentioned Ubangee's name, the first thing that came to mind were long, slim legs in stilettos, up to her armpits. HE was about to have a conversation and assign new duties to the four of them when Morris appeared.

Now was not the time but being who HE was, he listened to Morris. Morris was becoming one of HIS favorites though he would swear, HE never swore, he played no favorites.

"Sir, I know you have many, many important things on your mind and my needs are real low on your list, but I would really like to form a bowling league and there are no alleys. Is it possible that . . ."

"OF COURSE THERE ARE ALLYS. RIGHT OVER THERE ON CLOUD SEVENTEEN. THEY HAVE BEEN FRESHLY OILED, ALWAYS OPEN AND EVERYONE HAS HIS OWN CUSTOM-FIT BALL."

Morris was positive they were not there a minute ago but who was he to argue. He had what he asked for. Now to order some shirts.

"THE SHIRTS ARE THERE ALSO. WITH YOUR NAME EMBROYDERED ON THE FRONT. DON'T WORRY ABOUT SPONSORS, LIKE EVERYTHING ELSE HERE, IT'S ON THE HOUSE."

Morris could just picture Veronica with a short black skirt and a yellow bowling shirt tight across her bust. He knew she had great form and would be an excellent keggler.

I wonder how many teams there should be and who will be on mine.

Morris already decided he would be the team captain.

27

BOWLING ALLEYS. A DAMN GOOD IDEA EVEN IF I DIDN'T THINK OF IT MYSELF. NOT EVERYONE WANTS TO HANG OUT IN THE LIBRARY. WHAT ABOUT A THEME PARK. THAT WOULD BE FUN TO DO. I HAVE A FEW FREE HOURS IN THE MORNING TO DO IT. MAY JUST PEEK AND SEE WHAT DISNEY HAS DONE RECENTLY. DON'T WANT TO BE SECOND RATE, NOT WITH ALL THESE DAMN CRITICS UP HERE.

Kumbasa and Ubangee had been patiently waiting for HIM to give them their next assignment. Ubangee was becoming a bit self-conscious. HE was constantly staring at her legs. HE could have visually undressed her at any time and there was little she could do or say. She tried to tug her toga down a few inches. It did no good. She wished she had on some underwear.

Any kind of underwear.

SORRY. RULES ARE RULES.

Ubangee wondered why HE deemed it was not necessary. All HIS children were made in HIS likeness. She questioned that concept big time. HE was big but had lumbering legs that had little muscle tone.

Instinctively HE flexed HIS leg muscles. It did not do a great deal of good.

I HAVE TO START RUNNING AGAIN OR FIND A NEW PERSONAL TRAINER. THORPE IS GETTING FAT AND LAZY.

HE turned back to Kumbasa and Ubangee, who were now standing slightly behind him. Not that it would do any good if HE wanted to look.

"SORRY UBANGEE, I WAS NOT THINKING OF YOUR LEGS. SORRY IF I EMBARRASED YOU."

Ubangee pretended to smile.

"HOW WOULD THE TWO OF YOU LIKE TO GO TO BRAZIL? THEY ARE HAVING A MAJOR PROBLEM THERE. THE GUYS CAN'T STOP THINKING ABOUT IT. NEVER SHOULD HAVE ALLOWED THEM TO INVENT THOSE OUTRAGEOUS DANCES – AND OUTFITS."

Both Kumbasa and Ubangee blushed.

Ten minutes later they were in Rio de Janeiro. Ubangee was now wearing a colorful, if slightly immodest wraparound that showed off her legs to the fullest. Kumbasa was wearing a straw hat, blue shorts, a yellow, red and green shirt and looked like a native.

"I think we are going to have lots of fun here."

Kumbasa was already shaking his booty to the rhythm.

Ubangee agreed as she began to practice. She was a natural.

'**YOU ARE THERE TO WORK. YOU SHOULD BOTH BE WEARING PURE WHITE BUT I UNDERSTAND THE NEED TO FIT IN. I WILL COME UP WITH A PLAN IN A LITTLE WHILE. I HAVE TO BUILD A THEME PARK TOMORROW. HAVE FUN YOU TWO, BUT NOT TOO MUCH."**

The couple had no idea what HE was talking about. A theme park – UP THERE?

It was about that time HE overheard, HE was not purposely listening, as Morris was excitedly letting Veronica know she would be on his new bowling team, the TEN PIN KNOCKERS, as in knocking down the bowling pins. In addition to Veronica who everyone knew was well built and himself, he would invite Jane Russell and Jayne Mansfield. The only real questions were, one, could he find shirts to restrain their most noticeable features and two, would they have the ability to stand back up after releasing the ball.

HE was not pleased. This was supposed to be a recreational sport, not a new version of a wet tee shirt contest. HE decided he would have a little talk with Morris.

THE ETERNAL SHTUP

Surprisingly enough, the Brazilians were always up for something new, something different, something erotic. Esoteric love could / would be the new fad. They could / would have contests and winners would be matched up to compete at local, city, state and regional levels. The judges of course were Kumbasa and Ubangee. It was a competition between the men and women as to who had the most will power and self control. Teams were organized. Books and videos flooded the stores. Seminars by those who thought they knew, (they didn't have a clue) were conducted everywhere.

Within weeks the movie houses were taken over by E. L. contests. People fought to be included. Couples practiced at home, in the parks, on the beach. At restaurants. Everywhere. There were no restrictions. It became a national craze. Those under sixteen were excluded; it did not go over very well. Everyone wanted in. It did not lead to pregnancy, it did just the opposite. Why not allow the teeny boppers to participate. It could not hurt; it could only help.

Ubangee could not believe the outpour of contestants and contests. Special clothing was purchased, even more seductive than the already scandalous outfits worn by the ladies and young girls. An entire outfit could fit in the palm of one hand. Boys and men were wearing tight fitting pants to outline their somewhat altered and enlarged manhood. Dark sunglasses were mandatory. Heated Latino music was tailored with dramatic crescendo endings. It was all anyone heard.

The temperature went up a good ten degrees – everywhere.

The government was thinking of putting restrictions on the contests when they were reminded of the reason for them in the first place. To restrict the population growth. That's when the politicians realized this was a win / win situation. That was all that was heard on the TV or in the newspapers.

El Presidente announced at the end of sixty days there would be a national contest. It would be held on one of the most magnificent boardwalks in the entire world, Avenida Atlantica at Copacabana. There would be five couples competing, there would be grandstands for hundreds and of course, it would be carried on national television on a Saturday night. Along with the now suddenly enthusiastic *El Presidente,* the final decision would be made by Kumbasa and Ubangee.

Obviously, HE would be observing. Closely. Very closely.

IT IS WORKING; IT REALLY IS WORKING.

28

Kumbasa and Ubangee came home like conquering heroes.

HE could have not been more pleased. Everyone was talking. Marilyn and Bobby took a back seat to the activities and the parade. Although they were Chief Ambassadors at Large, they had never scored such a well televised, well publicized, well attended, event. Brazil was now a world leader. In fact they were THE leader in esoteric love. CNN, NBC and several European TV networks picked up the feed and ran with it. It was estimated more than sixty three million people worldwide saw the finals in Copacabana. The reruns ran for days and days. All told, more than two hundred fifty million saw the winner, Jose Carlos Vasquez; walk off with the three foot trophy and a check for 100,000 reals, about $40,000 U S.

Not bad for something he probably would have done at home for nothing.

It had been a cat and mouse game at the end. Three couples were eliminated in the first twenty minutes. The last two couples were playing it cagey. One couple was young and inexperienced so it came down to Esteletta and Jose Carlos, husband and wife, both clinical psychologists at Universidad de San Pablo.

Esteletta faked an orgasm. It didn't fool Jose. They had been married for close to fifteen years and he knew what was real and what was not. Jose had a plan; a well conceived plan. He let out a scream of joy, pretended to celebrate and proceeded to have one giant orgasm. He raised his hands in victory and waved to the cameras and the crowd. It was then Esteletta announced she in fact had not come, declared herself the winner and stood with both hands raised in victory. She then lay back, closed her eyes and confidently and enthusiastically masturbated to conclusion. She had a sheepish grin on her face. She had finally beaten her husband at his own game.

Jose said nothing. He too stood, pulled down his shorts and let the world see he still had an erection. He turned towards the TV camera and quickly and professionally finished what he had previously begun. Esteletta stared and knew she had been beaten. Then in front of the audience and at least a million viewers, he smiled and cleaned himself off.

The crowd went wild. The TV producer had scored a first. What was just telecast, live, had never been done before. At least never on national TV on prime time.

Ubangee waited till Jose Carlos was properly tucked back in before she handed him the phallic like trophy and the check.

Everyone in Brazil went wild.

THE ETERNAL SHTUP

Kumbasa and Ubangee accomplished far more than they ever could have imagined.

They went back home, heroes.

There are no ticker tape parades UP THERE, but if there were, HE would have been the driver of the open four-door Lincoln convertible and Ubangee and Kumbasa would have been sitting on top of the back seat smiling and waving to the cheering crowd.

UP THERE, victories like that were few and far between.

HE was now a most happy fella.

Ming Haw and Gintasa did not feel like celebrating. Sure they were all part of the same team but the old adage, "What have you done for me lately" hung heavy on their respective shoulders. Their success in Wuhan seemed like centuries ago. They needed to do something to upstage Ubangee and Kumbasa.

"But what?"

HE was listening. HE was always listening – and thinking.

HMM, THE CHINESE NEW YEAR IS RIGHT AROUD THE CORNER. THE GOVERNMENT IS BESIDE ITSELF WITH THE UNCONTROLLABLE POPULATION GROWTH. WHY DON'T I HAVE A LITTLE TALK WITH XI TAMPING, PRESIDENT OF THE PEOPLE'S REPUBLIC OF CHINA?

Xi Tamping had been taught not believe in HIM. HE did not trust XI. It was a perfect scenario. A Mexican standoff. They had what could be best described as a meeting of the minds. Each could claim victory; HE was not interested in scoring points or being reelected, and each would achieve what they had hoped for.

The meeting was held in the strictest of confidence on what appeared to be a simple sampan in the South China Sea. The interior was truly the lap of luxury. HE commented the tea and hospitality was excellent, especially on such short notice. HE especially liked the spring rolls with a generous helping of duck sauce. At times like these, HE regretted there were no restaurants UP THERE.

All terms were agreed upon. XI now knew where his final resting place would be.

A negotiated *quid pro quo*.

The next day or close to it, Ming Haw and Gintasa appeared in Guangzhou, one of the country's largest cities. They were introduced by none other than Xi Tamping, himself.

The square held more than 120,000 loyal but sorely discontent citizens. They were anxious to begin the celebration. It would be the Year of the Cat. The previous year had not been a good one. The people could not live on promises forever. It was more than a bit unusual for the president to make the opening remarks. People were fearful of more cutbacks, more restraints, less food to fill their shrunken bellies. More hours in government factories.

THE ETERNAL SHTUP

How many basketball shoes can those damn American wear?

Xi did not appear to have skipped any meals. If anything, he put on a few more pounds. There was no shortage of squid or other delicacies at the royal palace.

Another example of China's golden rule.

He who has the gold, rules.

The crowd stood silently and listened. They were not impressed, they were not enthusiastic. A chicken in every pot would have gone over far better. What good was sex without touching? It had to be some Communist trick. Both Ming Haw and Gintasa did their best to demonstrate and convince. It was like talking to the Great Wall itself. Xi was getting desperate. He had given his word. More important, he wanted his place reserved UP THERE. Sweat was beginning to form under his pristine tailored khaki uniform. The neck collar felt a bit too tight. Beads would shortly be seen on his high forehead. It was only seven degrees Celsius. He stepped to the microphone. The noisy crowd again became respectfully silent.

Xi had to think of something. Fast.

"For every year any married couple under the age of forty remains barren, they will receive sixty thousand Yuan in food stamps."

Dead silence as they all calculated. Everyone had a new AppleWatch with built-in calculators.

This was the equivalent of approximately $10,000 US.

Xi was also calculating. With a total population of more than 1.3 billion, there had to be at least 400,000 people between twenty and forty. That would mean close to 200,000 couples receiving $10,000 US per year. He had no idea where that kind of money would come from. All he knew, all he cared about was by the time they ran out of money or food stamps, he would be resting peaceably on Cloud Nine, Ten or Eleven. It would no longer be his problem. He looked out at the masses.

The audience was stunned. They looked at each other; they looked at Xi and then they looked again at Ming Haw and Gintasa. Sixty thousand Yuan was more than most of them made in four to five months in a sweatshop factory. And without feeding little ones, there was an enormous big pot of expendable income – there would even be enough for a month's vacation anywhere outside the steaming, hot city. Possibly a new car. And clothes and furniture.

Maybe a LG 65" TV.

The pot would again be full – and remain full.

Physical sex is not all it is cracked up to be.

This would be their new motto.

The crowd erupted with shouts of joy.

THE ETERNAL SHTUP

Ming How and Gintasa wondered how big THEIR parade would be.

"BIG. VERY, VERY BIG. THAT'S A PROMISE."

This time everyone smiled.

29

The Ambassadors of Love project had exceeded even HIS wildest expectations. It would take years but the handwriting was on the wall. There would be a down trend in the population explosion. The long term effects would be seen UP HERE in a hundred years. Maybe less. HE couldn't be happier and all because of Tiffany. HE had to do something to reward her, but what?

For now HE had time to concentrate on other matters.

AN AMUSEMENT PARK. BIGGER AND MORE SPECTATULAR THAN DISNEY. WHY NOT.

The first question is what type of rides? How and where and what?

Phineas Taylor Barnum had been hanging around doing practically nothing for the past one hundred twenty five years. He resented the phrase attributed to him, "There's a sucker born every minute" since he first heard it.

THE ETERNAL SHTUP

"I may have thought it, but never once said it. At least not out loud."

He did have a knack for finding ways of making people happy at amusement parks while deftly separating them from their hard earned money. P.T. spent his days following the progress of Mr. Walter Disney and his many successful, worldwide enterprises.

"GOOD MORNING P.T. DO YOU HAVE A FEW MINUTES TO TALK. I NEED A FAVOR. I NEED YOUR EXPERTISE."

Barnum was shocked HE even recognized him. What does HE want from me?

"GLAD YOU ASKED. PULL UP A BIT OF CLOUD AND LET'S TALK TURKEY."

P.T rubbed his palms. He was about to be back in the action. He was not forgotten and he would promise everyone would get their monies worth. And then some. There would be no suckers UP HERE.

HE explained.

"Sir, that is right up my midway. I have dozens of great ideas. I had them long before Walt or Roy even thought about them. But I did not have the technology back then and there were few who could afford to spend money on amusement rides. Let me explain what I have in mind."

HE smiled. It was now only a matter of time. A day or two at most. On the third day HE would rest. Maybe test out the new giant blue cloud sky coaster.

"SAFE, EXCITING AND FREE. OF COURSE, NO LINES, NO WAITING. PEOPLE DON'T LIKE TO WAIT NO MATTER HOW MUCH TIME THEY HAVE. YOU GOT THAT. THOSE ARE YOUR MARCHING ORDERS."

"Yes SIR."

PT grabbed a sheath of parchment paper, a few quill pens and buried himself in drawings. Typewriters were no good for what he had in mind. He had no use for computers or anything he did not understand. He would need the assistance of engineers and those types of people, but the ideas would be his and his alone.

HE will be pleased.

HE looked down and smiled. It was getting to be a habit; a very good habit.

HE decided he wanted a manager; someone to coordinate and report back to him. HE felt Morris would be good for the job. As his co manager, equal responsibilities although no pay to either; would be Veronica.

They were thrilled. Morris would again be a *gantser k'nacker,* a real big shot.

How do I improve on this?

THE ETERNAL SHTUP

"YOU DON'T MORRIS. YOU DON'T. YOU JUST MIND YOUR P'S & Q'S AND DO WHAT I TELL YOU TO DO."

So maybe I'm not such a big shot after all.

"GOOD THINKING MORRIS. NOW WE'RE ON THE SAME PAGE."

The park was not opened on time. There was a delay of close to twenty four hours. HE was not sure if it was the fault of the Teamsters or one of the other trade unions. There would be no announcement, no advertising, no Grand Opening celebration. It simply would be there for anyone to use. There were no lines, no tickets and certainly no waits.

There were also no children.

This had been something HE had wrestled with for the past ten thousand years; probably a great deal more. Newborns died during childbirth; infants died from lack of nutrition; babies died whenever there was a plague, small children died from neglect. That had been more than HE cared to think about.

THESES CHILDREN WOULD NEVER KNOW WHAT IT WOULD BE LIKE TO REACH MATURITY. TO LOVE AND BE LOVED AS ADULTS.

SO WHERE WILL THEY GO? WHAT WILL BECOME OF THEM?

HE had few regrets. Very few. The fact HE set a policy at the very beginning to not admit anyone UP HERE under the age of eighteen at the time of death, still bothered HIM. They had never understood the policy of death. Of what eternity truly meant. Their brains could not accept the difference between UP HERE and DOWN THERE. So they had their own space. It was a type of heaven where those under eighteen went. This space had no formal name and was seldom spoken of.

It was THE GOOD PLACE.

HE thought it would be a good idea to build a childproof, smaller version of the amusement park in THE GOOD PLACE. This time he would not use Barnum. HE would go directly to Wally. Who knew more about entertaining children than Roy himself?

Walter hated the nickname Wally, given to him by accident one weekend by his kid brother Roy.

Walt was thrilled. He was tired of all those animated movies. He wanted hands on, fear-in-the-eye, rides to excite and challenge the kids. Movies made money, a theme park brought smiles and tears and laughter and joy. The kids had more than their share of reality. In most cases they had not yet reached puberty and now they were dead. It was not their fault. They would never know the joy of being truly in love; of being loved by an equal. They would never know the joy of parenthood; they would never experience what it was like to have grandchildren of their own.

So many experiences they would never have. How unfair; how truly unfair.

THE ETERNAL SHTUP

IT WILL BE THE BEST KID'S AMUSMENT PARK ANYONE HAS EVER SEEN. IT WILL BE CALLED KIDS. KEEP IN DANGER FREE SITE, PARK.

Walt was now in his element. He called in those who could help him. He wanted ideas from everyone. This would be his best work – Ever.

HE was pleased. HE also knew he had to rethink his policy on kids. Maybe convene an advisory panel to make recommendations. It was a no win situation and HE knew it. For now KIDS PARK was paramount.

While thinking about the park it occurred to him, he had not thought about a mate/partner/companion in some time. HE was not sure if that was bad or good. HE would think about it, just not now.

At that moment a couple of young dollies flirted by. They were no more than eighteen, nineteen at the most and their togas were a tad too short, their cleavage a bit too exposed and their smiles a bit too suggestive for public decency.

DON'T THEY KNOW WHERE THEY ARE?

He said nothing. HE was not sure how much good it would do anyway.

KIDS. CAN'T CONTROL THEM ANYMORE. I REMEMBER WHEN I WAS A . . .

Walt was standing there. Obviously with a question.

HE never finished his thought. Probably a good thing.

A COMMITTEE, YES I'LL CONVENE A COMMITTEE. LET THEM HANDLE THE PROBLEM. ALWAYS A GOOD WAY TO RESOLVE ANY STICKY SITUATION.

Walt was still waiting.

He would just have to wait a little longer.

30

HE decided to follow the dollies or at least find out what they were up to. If it looks like trouble, if it smells like trouble, if it sounds like trouble, even UP HERE, chances are it WAS trouble.

The dollies were named Betty and Veronica. No, not Morris's Veronica. They were much too young, much too promiscuous, much too bodacious and much too anxious, for their own good.

DEFINITELY A BAD COMBINATION.

There are few rules UP HERE. There is no law about being horny. It was one of the most natural instincts known to man – and woman. But a bit of discretion never hurt anyone. There is no booze of any kind and certainly no weed UP HERE. How the girls scored some grass, was a mystery. The fact was, they were sharing a doobie. A big giant doobie. No doubt about it. You could smell its pungent odor three clouds away. It smelled like Maui Wowy.

THAT'S A BIG GIANT NO NO. I WONDER WHAT OTHER TROUBLE THEY PLAN ON GETTING INTO?

It did not take HIM long to find out. They were heading for the bowling alley. The one Morris requested. There would be league games all evening. Morris was sure to be there. So would his own Veronica together with Jane and Jayne. Too healthy a combination for their own good.

THIS IS MY KINGDOM. NOTHING, AND I DO MEAN NOTHING, TAKES PLACE HERE WITHOUT MY KNOWLEDGE – AND CONSENT.

HE was becoming a bit upset.

It soon became obvious the girls were not there to bowl. They were there to hang out. There were no bars, no shopping malls, no Starbucks or Panera Bread or places to meet people; people their own age. More important, there were no iphones, or computers with sites like J Date, Match.com, e Harmony or Christian Mingle to meet new and similarly minded friends. They could not text naked pictures of themselves to their ex boyfriends to score some points and get a hot date. UP HERE was a whole new concept. One they had not thought of; one they had not prepared for. One they had hoped was a million years away.

Or at least fifty or sixty.

Betty and Veronica were not bad kids. They were just lonely and bored. Not a great combination. They were both killed the night of their high school prom. The driver and his buddy survived. The boys were too drunk to tense up and get fatally hurt. They ended up with multiple scratches, a whole bunch of broken bones, a badly bruised ego and in one case, a citation for DWI.

Four months earlier and the girls would have spent eternity in the GOOD PLACE.

Whether it was fortunate or not, they were now both HERE.

Morris and Veronica #1 did not know either of them. There were no restrictions at the alley. Everyone was welcome. Betty began to flirt. She was sending undeniable messages to the guys. She had nothing better to do. She was also very horny. She had 'gone all the way' not an hour before the car crash. The four of them left the prom a few minutes early and Betty and her date ended up in the back seat of a three year old Ford sedan. It was cramped and smelly, like her date had used it for the same purpose before. It was officially owned by her date's father but he had total access to it.

It was her first - and last time.

Now she wanted more.

"THERE ARE RULES HERE YOUNG LADY. A PROPER, PLACE, A PROPER TIME, A PROPER PARTNER. PLEASE REMEMBER WHERE YOU ARE. THIS IS NOT SOME DANK DIRTY DIVE."

Betty almost had a coronary. She had never heard HIM speak before. Certainly not to her. She began to sob and apologize and wanted to go home to her mother and family. Even

Timmy, her obnoxious little brother. She was too young to be HERE. She had made a mistake and she was sorry. She wanted to go back. She wanted to graduate high school with the rest of her class and go to college. She missed her friends.

"It's not fair. Do you hear me? It's just not fair."

"NO IT ISN'T. BUT IT'S TOO LATE FOR REGRETS. SORRY BETTY."

"Please, please. I promise I'll be good. I swear to. . .", she hesitated. She was afraid to speak HIS name.

There was no response. What was there to say?

Veronica, not Morris' Veronica, came over and put an arm around her shoulder. She too was on the verge of tears. She had already been accepted to a state university not far from home. It was not her first choice, not that it made any difference now. Her father had warned her about drinking and boys and prom nights. It was now too late.

Way too late.

How long do we have to stay here? When can we go home? When can I start classes? I want to be a dental hygienist so people can have germ free mouths and smiling teeth and be happy who they are and how they look.

Betty had read that in the school brochure.

"NEVER. THIS IS IT. FOREVER."

THE ETERNAL SHTUP

Veronica heard the words but could not accept what they meant. She could not stay here forever.

"What about all my friends? We are all supposed to go to New York City this summer for seven days. It is all arranged. I even have most of the money and I can earn the rest in a month or two."

"SORRY BETTY."

HE hated this part of the job. Under special circumstances, like the Ambassadors of Love, the Right of Return was granted but for only limited periods of time and under strict supervision. The chances of Betty and Veronica returning, even for one day, were absolutely zero. HE did not have the heart to tell the girls that. They would soon find out themselves. They would learn to accept the routine and be happy to be in HIS presence. That was the best that could be hoped for.

When Morris suggested they get fitted for a custom bowling ball, they cried in unison and stumbled to the door.

"Not fair; not fair" they wailed.

The bowling alley was deathly quiet. Everyone could feel their pain. They could also feel their own pain. No one was really ready for the transition. No matter how pleasant it was painted to be.

Morris picked up his ball and promptly threw it into the gutter. His mind was not on rolling a three hundred. His mind was not on his own Veronica. His mind was not even on his last days on earth at the Hospice of Boca Raton. All he could think about were two eighteen year old girls who were in the wrong place at the wrong time.

"I'm sorry," he quietly mumbled to absolutely no one at all.

HE was now on to other matters. One's he could control with less grief and sorrow.

NO ONE REALLY UNDERSTANDS WHAT THIS JOB IS ALL ABOUT. TRUST ME, IT'S NOT ALL SUNSHINE AND ROSES.

31

Betty sat by herself and thought. She thought about her mother and father who fought with each other way too much. She thought about Timmy who could be a real pain in the butt but who she loved very much. She even thought about Sparkle, her white fluffy little mutt she rescued from the SPCA a few years ago. She loved them all and she knew, in her heart of hearts, she would never see any of them again. At least not on earth.

Why me?

She knew at times she had been nasty to her mother, she had lied to her father about the boy she was dating, she had cheated on a take home exam and had copied almost three full pages on an essay she did not have time to research and write herself. These were all bad things but was it bad enough that she had to die and go to UP HERE without experiencing everything a teenager is suppose to.

Yes, I had sex. Once. It was not that great. In fact it hurt like hell and my date had no idea what he was doing. Well he had some idea but he was all thumbs and apologies. I've had never really been in love. Not the kind of love I read about in books or saw on the TV. Someday I want a baby. My own baby I can feed and nurse and change its diapers and love it unconditionally. If it's a girl I will make sure she does not make the same mistakes I made.

Betty had promised herself she would go to college, graduate, get her degree and make something of herself. Then and only then would she find a husband. Someone who loved her for what she was, not what she could do for him. She wanted two children, a boy and girl, not a whole slew of them taking up all her time and effort and love.

Two would be just the right number.

That's never going to happen now. All because I got in a car with someone I knew had been drinking too much. I can't believe I am here – forever, because of one stupid mistake in judgment. One lousy mistake. Just one.

HE heard and wanted to correct the problem. HE had the ultimate authority. No one could question HIM.

BUT WHAT PRESCEDENT WOULD IT SET. I JUST CANNOT DO IT. IF I BEND THE RULES FOR BETTY, WHO WOULD BE NEXT?

After a few seconds to reflect, HIS answer stood.

RULES ARE RULES.

THE ETERNAL SHTUP

While sitting and feeling sorry for herself, Betty was approached by one of the most handsome young men she had ever seen. He was tall, lean, had a pompadour haircut and wearing a perfect collar, white tee shirt and brown leather motorcycle jacket. Not exactly approved clothing for UP HERE. He obviously was a rebel. He had an unlit cigarette behind his left ear that looked like it had been there for years. It had. Ever since he died in the fiery auto accident in his then brand new white Porsche 550 Spyder. He had a look about him as if he was resigned as to his fate.

"What seems to be the problem Sweet Lips?"

Betty blushed.

"Do I know you? Your face looks sort of familiar. I think maybe from an old time poster."

"Hope it was not too old. I died in Hollywood in 1955. Just when I had made it big."

"What's your name?"

Betty was getting excited. For the first time since "the accident".

He seemed to hesitate. He wanted to talk for a few minutes before he told her. He wanted to see if she liked him or who he had been.

"How'd a young girl like you get up here so early?"

"Auto accident."

He frowned. "Me too. I was driving near L.A., a Ford on the other side of the road crossed the center line and we had a head on collision. Next thing you know, here I am."

He took out a comb from his rear pocket and slicked back his hair in a D A, a ducks ass haircut.

"Can't blame no one. Was my fault. Not real familiar with the wheels."

"So, what's your name? Or are you ashamed of it."

"Whoa. For a young girl who has not been here very long, you've got a few things to learn about that sassy mouth of yours. My name's James Dean. I was a movie star once upon a time. Ever see *Rebel Without A Cause*, or *Giant* or *East of Eden*? Nothing to be ashamed of about those flicks. People DOWN THERE still talk about them. Damn good, if I must say so myself."

Betty gasped. She had never seen any of the movies but she had seen his posters – everywhere. Why he was a true cultural icon. He was the very essence of teenage disillusionment. And he died the same way she had.

"Mr. Dean. I'm sorry I said that. So, so sorry."

"Please call me Jimmy. My few close friends did. Before I got here."

THE ETERNAL SHTUP

"Alright JIMMY."

"Let's go for a walk. Too many eyes around here."

With that he took her hand in his and began walking at a brisk pace. She had trouble keeping up with him.

"Slow down, please."

"Never," he replied.

I COULDN'T HAVE PLANNED THAT ANY BETTER IF I TRIED.

The last HE saw of them, they were off Cloud Eight, heading towards Nine.

MAYBE SHE'LL BE HAPPY NOW. JAMES HAS A WAY OF DOING THAT FOR THE NEWBIES.

The fact was, James had made it a habit of introducing himself to those unfortunate young ladies who had arrived much too soon. It was his private welcoming party and he had no devious intentions, despite the ever prominent rumors.

Earth, heaven, hell, there were always rumors.

He knew all too well what it was like to be called away before his time. He was only twenty four and had the whole world ahead of him. This was his way of making the transition a little bit easier for them.

As they walked and talked they became more comfortable with each other. The ball of fire car crash stirred unimaginable memories for both of them. Waking up HERE, not knowing how or what, was an experience no one wanted to have. The rules upon entering were vague to say the least.

They sat and rested. He was still holding her hand. She liked it. She more than liked it. She asked dozens of questions; he tried to answer all of them. No one told him what to expect once he was UP HERE. No one gave him a manual or introductory course on what to expect — and what was expected from him. It was new and confusing and more than a bit frightened. He did not know what the rules were or if there were any.

"Maybe we can organize a teen, post teen, welcoming party. Sort of like college orientation, though neither of us has ever been to college. We could introduce them to others who died young and make them feel this really is their new home — forever."

Betty liked the idea. She was thinking of Veronica who she always called Ronnie. It would give Ronnie something to do and get her out of her funk.

WHY DIDN'T I THINK OF THAT? I CAN'T POSSIBLY THINK OF EVERYTHING, CAN I?

HE immediately gave his blessings.

"I think it's a fab idea. Let's do it. I can't wait to tell Ronnie about it. And all about you. A real movie star."

THE ETERNAL SHTUP

Betty was about to say *real live movie star*, but that would not have been quite true.

The ball began to roll. It picked up steam. Before you knew it, hundreds of recently departed / recently arrived young individuals were anxious to participate. They were from eighteen, the minimum legal age to their mid twenties. There were more than a few military men and women, all taken without just cause.

WHAT A SHAME. WHAT A TRAVESTY. AND TO THINK MOST WARS ARE FOUGHT IN MY NAME. HOW ABSURD. HOW BARBARIC, HOW UNETHICAL. HOW WRONG. WAR DOES NOT BRING PEACE. ONLY PEACE BEGETS MORE PEACE. LOVE THY BROTHER AS YOU WOULD LOVE THYSELF

A tear formed in HIS eye.

A ringing chorus of Hallelujah was heard in the background.

32

Morris again wondered about marriage. Veronica had never mentioned it. It was totally his idea. Was it necessary? Who would know? Who would care? Was it expected? He was not sure. Was it even done? He had not seen any chapels or Vegas style drive thrus. There were no wedding dress shops. Or even tux rentals. What about flowers and a reception hall? Where there good caterers? Are there any caterers?

"THERE IS NO FOOD HERE. WHY WOULD I HAVE CATERERS? THINK MORRIS, THINK."

Morris felt sheepish. He was not thinking.

What about invitations, photographers, a place to have the ceremony.

It was all so time consuming. And if there was no money, who would do it and how would they get paid? All good questions. No good answers. What about presents? There were no stores to buy gifts. Who would he invite and who would be left out? What about the band and the type of music they would play. Morris had heard Woody Herman, Guy Lombardo were both available.

Morris assumed if there were weddings, HE would officiate.

Would it be on a Saturday or a Sunday and who knew the difference.

I DON'T DO WEDDINGS OR BAR MITZVAHS, MORRIS

From time to time Morris saw rabbis or what he assumed were rabbis. They dressed in long black coats, all had beards and payus, wide brimmed black hats and carrying what looked like the bible. The Old Testament,of course. Morris was not sure how much authority, if any, they had.

Better I should ask the Boss.

It was time for another talk. Morris knew HE could always spare a few minutes for his buddy. After all, HE was his BFF.

"YES MORRIS, WHAT CAN I DO FOR YOU NOW?"

It was not as if Morris was his only worry.

Morris explained his situation – Ad Nauseum.

"MORRIS SWEETHEART. WHY THE BIG *SIMUS*. VERONICA IS NEVER GOING TO GET PREGNANT SO THERE IS NO WORRY ABOUT CHILDREN OR WHAT RELIGION THEY WILL BE BROUGHT UP IN. THERE ARE NO DIVORCES AND THANKS TO ME, NO DIVORCE LAWYERS. REAL ESTATE AND PROBATE

LAWYERS, YES. DIVORCE LAWYERS, NO. IF YOU ARE LIVING IN HERE, YOU CERTAINLY CAN NOT BE LIVING IN SIN. YOU ARE BOTH CONSENTING ADULTS, I ASSUME SHE IS CONSENTING, SO WHY MAKE A BIG DEAL OF THIS. STOP WORRYING YOUR *KEPALA* OFF. GO, ENJOY, FORNICATE AND BE HAPPY. HAVE A NICE DAY."

HE enjoyed practicing his Yiddish whenever he got the opportunity. Morris appreciated the sound advice and thanked HIM profusely. It had taken a big load off his mind.

"I spoke to HIM. HE said not to worry. Marriage is a concept only on Earth, not here. Besides, there is no place to buy a trousseau. And where would we go on a honeymoon. We are already here.

Veronica began to cry. They were tears of happiness. Morris panicked. He would never understand women. Not before, not now, not ever.

"Did I say something wrong?"

"No. you're wonderful."

Morris felt good and had no idea why.

"You think maybe we could fool around a little. Sort of celebrate whatever I did right."

"No time like the present."

THE ETERNAL SHTUP

Before he could comment they were back in the bedroom. Morris was not sure whose bedroom it was, not that it really made a difference. Veronica was now standing in front of him with both arms raised.

Her smile told him everything he needed to know.

"Please undress me."

She was only wearing a lightweight summer toga.

He took the toga by the hem and raised it above her head. It fell innocently to the floor. Morris assumed it was the floor. He could never be sure.

"Let's pretend we're going to make a baby."

Morris was very good at 'Let's pretend'.

HE took the credit for that one.

IT SEEMS LIKE EVERYONE IS DOING IT – EXCEPT ME.

For the first time in millenniums, HE became embarrassed.

I OBVIOUSLY NEED A PARTNER. BUT WHO?

As he was contemplating the question, a most striking lady walked briskly by and never bothered to acknowledge HIS presence. It was as if she did not recognize HIM or did not care. That in itself drew his attention. It was not a question of being arrogant or needing recognition, he knew who he was, but it was rather unusual for one to walk by, almost bumping into HIM, without as much as a salutation.

WHO IS SHE?

Normally HE had total recall but for some reason today, HIS mind went blank. At least blank as to her name. The face was all too familiar. He knew he could not be having a senior moment. HE did not have senior moments. Not now, not ever.

HE was not about to ask anyone. That would have been even more embarrassing.

HE took a couple of quick steps and caught up to her. She was wearing the typical white with gold trim Greek style toga. No help there. HE had the distinct feeling something had changed about her. Something was different. She walked with a purpose. Exasperated, he took the initiative and walked directly up to her. She was neither startled nor frightened.

Annoyed would be a better description.

"I'M SORRY; I DON'T SEEM TO REMEMBER HOW LONG YOU HAVE BEEN WITH US. COULD YOU PLEASE ENLIGHTEN ME.?"

"Nineteen hundred sixty eight. June first, if you must know the exact date. I was eighty eight when I died. If you will excuse me, I have work to do at the library. Now that I have regained my hearing and sight, thank God, I have a great deal of catching up to do."

It suddenly occurred to HIM; she had no idea who HE was. It also occurred to HIM as to who she was.

"MISS KELLER?"

"Yes, what is it now?"

HE could tell she was not pleased to be questioned again.

"I DID NOT MEAN TO BOTHER YOU. I MUST ADMIT I DID NOT RECOGNIZE YOU. YOU LOOK SO MUCH DIFFERENET THESE DAYS."

"Now that I've been given back all my senses, or that I don't need a damn dog or aide to hover over me 24/7, life, well I guess I should say, afterlife, is a blast. And you are?"

"SORRY I DID NOT INTRODUCE MYSELF. I'M GOD."

"Right. Sure you are. And I'm horny old Mother Theresa. Nice to meet you."

'NO YOU'RE NOT. YOU'RE HELEN KELLER, THE WRITER."

"You got me there friend. Yes I am. By the way, I'm also a former member of the American Socialist Party, champion of labor rights and women's suffrage. Let's give a little credit where credit is due. I worked my ass off to get an education with all those huge road blocks HE threw in front of me."

"MS KELLER, I REALLY AM GOD. ASK ANYONE."

"Really? Had I known you sooner maybe I would have been able to see and hear and I wouldn't have spent the last fifty years of my life bumping into things. Just look at my chins and ankles. I thought they would never heal. And do you have any idea what it was like to sleep next to Kamikaze Go, that Akita of mine that farted all night long for more than fifteen years. Not exactly paradise. And while I'm at it, I have a few bones to pick with YOU. Making me blind was not enough; you had to make me deaf also. What kind of sick joke is that? Now you're telling me you really are GOD and all this was something of a practical joke? Give me a freakin break."

"PLEASE HELEN, I CAN EXPLAIN."

"Well it had better be good. I'm surprised you didn't make me a cripple also. Sort of like the old hat trick. Sit down and make yourself comfortable. I've been waiting forty-five years to give YOU a piece of my mind and hear, by the way, YOU do know I can now hear, don't YOU, why YOU thought this would have made me a better person? I'm listening."

"I UNDERSTAND - BUT I HAVE A PRESSING APPOINTMENT."

"The appointment is just going to have to wait Buster. I have a list here," she reached under her ill fitting toga for a shopping list of complaints, "and YOU'RE going nowhere till I get this off my chest. Understand! Now don't argue with me and sit."

THE ETERNAL SHTUP

HE sat. And listened. And listened.

Helen was in no hurry to go anywhere. She had a laundry list of complaints.

Everyone walking anywhere near the library took a wide berth of the two of them. It looked like HE was in for a long afternoon.

A very long afternoon.

33

HE could not apologize more profusely. It was a mistake. No one deserves to lose two of their senses. One was bad enough. It had to be a computer glitch. Some type of computer malfunction.

Helen was not buying into any of it. There were no computers when I was born. HE or one of HIS associates, screwed up.

"How would YOU feel if the tables were turned?"

HE had no answer.

"I'M NOT SURE HOW, BUT I'LL MAKE IT UP. JUST GIVE ME A DAY OR TWO. AND AGAIN, I'M SORRY FOR THE MAJOR SCREW UP."

Helen was not about to let HIM off the hook so easily.

"Eighty eight freakin years of being blind and deaf. Do you have any idea how that put a cramp in my style? As to sex, I had no idea who or what I was doing most of the time. A real double klutz. What was I to do when someone grabbed a quick feel? Yell, scream, slap him? I had no idea who it was. God only knows, sorry about that slip, who I was screwing. I couldn't let out a scream for joy when I had a giant orgasm. How do you think the guy felt? Like he was schtupping a real dummy. All thanks to YOU."

HE remained silent. Better to have her let it all out.

"Most of the time I felt like an idiot and could not even hear or see people laughing at me when I fell down or walked into something. Whatever YOU have in mind, it had better be damn good. I'm not settling for some stuffed teddy bear or a damn carnival kewpie doll."

"I PROMISE; I PROMISE."

HE was now thinking, **HOW DO I MAKE UP FOR THAT SNAFU?**

"Don't you dare run away from me. I'm not finished with you yet."

"I'M GOING NOWHERE. WE'LL TALK MORE TOMORROW."

For a minute, HE thought he had met his match.

SHE'S ONE HELL OF A FIESTY BROAD, HE thought.

And she certainly was.

Morris, as had a couple of dozen voyeurs, had been watching the confrontation from a safe distance. They actually felt sorry for HIM. HE couldn't walk away fast enough. This had to be a first, some thought.

It was.

"Excuse me SIR, I couldn't help but overhear Ms. Keller talking to you. YOU promised you would do something to make it up to her in a day or two."

HE was not in a particularly good mood and did not need Morris to remind him of promises he had made.

DON'T PEOPLE KNOW WHO I AM? DO THEY REALLY THINK I FORGET SO EASILY?

"YES MORRIS, I REMEMBER. AND HOW IS THIS OF ANY INTEREST TO YOU?"

HE was getting a touch feisty himself.

"Well I think I can help. You know, find something that would make Ms. Keller pleased after the computer glitch or whatever caused the 'double'".

HE did not like the term, "The Double'. HE was about to tell Morris to mind his own business when it came to HIM. Give Morris a chance. Like chicken soup, it may not help, but it couldn't hurt.

THE ETERNAL SHTUP

"YOU'VE GOT FORTY EIGHT HOURS, GIVE IT YOUR BEST SHOT MORRIS"

HE knew forty eight hours meant nothing. It could be the time it takes to have a fresh thought or as long as it could take to solve the Arab / Israeli situation.

Namely forever.

Morris nodded and smiled. He had work to do and was not sure where to start. As usual, he spoke before he thought.

He then thought about the joke of HIM walking around with a white lab coat and stethoscope and the comment made.

"That's not a doctor. That's God, he just thinks he's a doctor."

Morris had his answer.

Betty and James were totally unaware of the confrontation that was now the talk of the place. They were off in their own little world, actually a small, unoccupied cloud a few minutes away. Betty was asking him questions that at times bordered on highly personal. Jimmy was not taken back by any of them. He had nothing to hide.

"Maybe it was ego, maybe it was a lack of self confidence but you can't let them see you sweat. If you don't believe in yourself, who will?"

She really wanted to get to know him better but was not sure if being a bit too aggressive was the right answer. She thought about what IT would be like. She was getting excited.

"Of course I want to make love to you. Why wouldn't I? You're sweet and caring, intelligent, beautiful and have a very inviting body. Besides, it's something you really want to do."

Betty blushed.

How does he know?

"Betty. There are no secrets UP HERE. We all know what each other are thinking and right now you must know that I am thinking I would very much like to help you remove your toga."

Betty squeezed her eyes closed and grinned.

I'm going to make love to James Dean. James Dean the movie star.

"Yes you are. Only make that former movie star."

And so they did.

While Betty and James were getting to know each other on a far more intimate level, Morris made up his mind what Helen really wanted. Now all he had to do was make the necessary arrangements.

THE ETERNAL SHTUP

Anything is possible UP HERE. Anything.

Helen could not believe it. It never occurred to her; she would never have made such a request but now that it was done; she still didn't understand how, she was thrilled.

Her only regret she did not have a mirror or a cell phone camera. She wanted to take a few selfies and send them to the world. To the universe, the entire galaxy. Helen now looked thirty years old, high cheek bones and sensuous lips. Every feature on her now radiant face had been sculptured by a true artist. UP HERE was loaded with top plastic surgeons and the most famous sculptures the world had ever known. Her bust size was several inches bigger and her waist a few inches smaller. She seemed to be a few inches taller. Her hair was now auburn and hung to her shoulders.

Helen Keller was now radiant. She was beautiful. She had been molded into a classic Greek princess. She couldn't wait to thank HIM. She purposely tightened the bust line a little bit, arched her back, straightened her shoulders and walked towards the library with an air of confidence never demonstrated before. Walking may be the wrong word. Strutting would be far more accurate.

"Morning Helen."

"Lovely day, Ms. Keller."

"You look absolutely fabulous my dear," came from none other than Zsa-Zsa Gabor

Helen accentuated her stride. One leg crossing over towards the other. You would have thought she was a Victoria's Secret runway model.

She sure felt like it.

HE actually stopped in HIS tracks. Someone new and delicious had arrived. And HE had not been notified. HE was about to call the front gate when Helen approached HIM.

"Thank you. YOU actually did come through on your promise. I must admit, I never dreamed of looking like this."

Helen took a deep breath filling her lungs to capacity and threw back her shoulders even farther.

"You're a sweetheart."

With that Ms. Keller planted one on HIS cheek.

HE was totally flustered.

"YOU'RE MOST WELCOME."

HE had no idea who he was talking to or why he was accepting her gratitude.

ALL IN A DAY'S WORK. I AM HERE TO MAKE PEOPLE HAPPY, EVEN IF AT TIMES I DON'T KNOW WHY.

Morris was beaming. He had done good. He would wait until later before speaking to HIM about what he had done.

THE ETERNAL SHTUP

The NEW Ms. Helen Keller headed up the library steps to the admiration of one and all.

It was worth it, damn it, it was all worth it.

Well, almost.

34

Ronnie was jealous.

Betty was off on some cloud bopping James Dean and she was sitting alone on a small cloud feeling sorry for herself. It was not as if she wished Betty anything but the very best, but a hunk like James Dean. Who would'a thought it?

It's not fair. We are BFF, we always double dated, we picked out our prom dresses together and made a pact; we would tell each other everything that happened after the prom, the next day. There never was a next day. One minute Ralphie had one arm around me, trying for a quick feel and the other on the wheel trying to avoid a set of headlights coming at us and the next thing I know, I'm UP HERE. Now Betty is off with a movie star and what do I do? Nothing. It's just not fair.

It was not done on purpose, but HE overheard the entire soliloquy.

I'VE GOT THE PERFECT GUY FOR RONNIE. WHAT'S HIS NAME? HE PLAYED PLATO OPPOSITE DEAN IN REBEL WITHOUT A

THE ETERNAL SHTUP

CAUSE. THE ITALIAN KID WHO WAS MURDERED BEHIND HIS APARTMENT IN NEW YORK IN THE LATE 60'S. HE WAS ONLY THIRTY SEVEN YEARS OLD. THEY CALLED HIM THE SWITCHBLADE KID. SEXY, LONELY, ALOOF. MINEO. THAT'S IT, SAL MINEO.

"Hi, looks like you could use a new friend. Want to talk about it?"

Ronnie looked up, saw Sal Mineo and promptly fainted.

It was not by coincidence the four of them bumped into each other. Sal and Ronnie were engaged in deep conversation about how he was murdered; it had nothing to do with his 'coming out' when they turned the corner and ran into Betty and James.

HE had to laugh, to himself of course, when he saw the expressions on all four of their faces. HE had planned it that way. HE did have a strange sense of humor. Some would say warped, but never out loud.

"How did you two, where did . . ."

"We met like you two met. It makes sense, you and I were in a number of movies together and hung out at times and Betty and Ronnie are Best Friends Forever. So why not."

They all looked at Sal. What he said made perfect sense. Ronnie was having a tough time picturing him as gay, not that it made any difference. All she wanted was to hang out with someone cool. Who could be any cooler than Sal Mineo?

"NO ONE. ABSOLUTELY NO ONE."

The four of them looked toward one of the high clouds and all whispered, "Thank you."

"YOUR WELCOME"

They had a great deal to be thankful for and all the time in the universe to enjoy each other's company.

"It doesn't get any better than this. Let's go race Go carts at the new amusement park"

The three of them looked at Ronnie and agreed.

HE looked down from where he now was and smiled.

It had nothing to do with Go carts or how many of HIS people enjoyed the park.

EVERYONE HAS SOMEONE – EXCEPT ME.

No secrets means, well no secrets.

RFK and Marilyn were now hanging out. They had no assignments recently and were talking about Obama or as Bobby liked to say, 44 Black, like a quarterback calling out a play. It never occurred to him when he was Attorney General, working for civil rights, for voting privileges, for equality, that one day a black man would sit where his brother had run the show.

THE ETERNAL SHTUP

"Unbelievable. Jack and I really did do some good. Who knows, maybe someday a Jew?"

"WE SHALL SEE. THEY'VE PACKED THE SUPREME COURT. NOW YOU WANT THE EXECUTIVE BRANCH TOO."

Morris, who had been standing nearby checking out Marilyn's boobs, shook his head. Everyone knew he was shading his eyes and looking down her toga, not squinting due to the sun.

The grass is always greener; the boobs are always bigger...

"Naw. There are more blacks than Jews. We'll never get a majority. Besides, there's more money in pulling the strings than being the puppet. He was thinking of arms dealers, defense contractors, and suppliers of foreign aid. The recent multibillion dollar budget for aid package to three African nations for commodes netted the contractor more than two hundred seventy million in profit alone. The toilet paper was marked up three hundred fifty percent. They had enough sent to wipe their asses for the next two hundred years.

The commodes were made in Taiwan, right around the corner, shipped to America and then sent on to West Africa. Almost full circle. And who do you think was behind the whole deal? A Jewish senator from New York and a Jewish wholesaler from Miami. Being president was small potatoes, no matter how much an ex president would charge for giving a thirty minute speech, eating some boiled chicken and shaking hands with those who were willing to pay big for a few not so small favors.

Slick Willie Clinton should have learned that a long time ago. One sweet deal in Bogota, South America could keep him in the lap of luxury, if you get my drift, for the rest of his life. Hillary would have happily arranged it for him, if anyone had asked.

No, being a politician is no big deal. Owning a politician, controlling a big name politician, now that's where the real gelt is.

Morris then remembered why he wanted to talk to Bobby. It was about HIM and "everyone has someone – except HIM".

"Bobby, I need your help. You must know someone to fix HIM up with. You're BIC, I'm not."

Kennedy smiled. He had not heard that expression in almost fifty years. B I C. Boston, Irish, Catholic.

His granddaddy, Honey Fitz, had taught him well, as to everything.

No one has ever asked me to get a date for HIM.

Talk about pressure, Bobby had his work cut out for him.

Maybe Jack has some suggestions.

I DON'T NEED ANY HELP. ESPECIALLY FROM A KENNEDY. I'LL JUST HAVE TO TELL THE BOYS TO MIND THEIR OWN BUSINESS.

THE ETERNAL SHTUP

JFK had to laugh.

"I won the election to become president of the United States of American without any help from HIM."

Morris wanted no part of this battle. He would find someone else to help him. Maybe Marty. Martin Luther King never had a problem meeting willing, cooperative and understanding young ladies.

As he headed towards the library Morris saw the usual crowd just hanging around. Off to the side was MLK with a group of young people. There appeared to be more young ladies than gentlemen. King had heard HE had befriended Morris, sort of like Facebook, and waved for him to come over.

"Can we talk Mr. King?"

"Of course, and please call me Marty."

The crowd quickly disbursed when they realized King was on to new business. Now Marty and Morris sat on the soft, almost padded like steps that looked like concrete and had a conversation. Obviously the conversation was about HIM and HIS needs.

HE listened to every word and was not pleased.

WHAT DO THEY THINK, THAT I CAN'T RESOLVE MY OWN PROBLEMS? THAT I'M SOME TYPE OF NEEDY PERSON. I APPREACIATE THEIR CONCERN BUT THIS IS WAY OUT OF

LINE. I DON'T NEED THE ENTIRE UNIVERSE TO KNOW WHAT I'M DOING – OR NOT DOING.

Without so much as an afterthought, HE grabbed a medium sized lightning bolt and flung it at a small cloud hovering above the library. It immediately began to rain. Exactly over the spot where Marty and Morris were sitting.

The two of them ran inside for cover.

THAT SHOULD END SUCH FOOLISHNESS.

Morris got the message. It may have temporarily deterred him but that would not stop him. HE needs help and refuses to ask.

"MORRIS, FOR MY SAKE, LEAVE IT ALONE."

Morris refused to even think about it. A thought was the same as a billboard across from the library as far as he was concerned.

There are no secrets here. I can't even think without HIM knowing it.

"THAT'S A FACT, JACK."

Morris knew he couldn't win. But he couldn't help trying.

What do I have to lose?

Morris had no idea.

35

Everyone knows UP HERE, all is peaceful, all is forgiven. It is made up of love and compassion and warm fuzzy feelings. That is what HE preaches. That is what is expected.

Not all the good citizens had the eternal love of HIM in their hearts

Jeanne d'Arc was born in Domremy, in the northeastern providence of France in 1412. Her parents were peasant folk. Jeanne died on May 30, 1431 in what was called the greatest injustice of the entire Middle Ages.

A musket to the heart kills within seconds. As to the guillotine, by the time the brain receives the impulse, the head is no longer part of the body. Burning at the stake takes forever. Why it takes close to three hours for the body to turn to ashes. How could HE do that to me? Did HE have any idea how long I was tied to that pillar before I actually died? The pain was unbelieable. I could not breathe and the meat was falling of my bones like smoked ribs at a barbecue joint. I was screaming but no one heard or cared. Not even HIM.

What about the fact that twenty-five years later I was exonerated. Totally exonerated. As in found not guilty.

Joan of Arc, the name and person most associated with the insidious deed, began hearing voices when she was thirteen years old. She was told it was her mission to save France. She did what she believed what was her calling. Six years later she was tried for witchcraft and heresy. She died in Vieux – Marche in Rouen, France.

Everyone tells me HE is a compassionate G-d. A loving G-d. One who loves all HIS children. What about me? Was I just chopped liver? Was HE too busy watching the Crusades on a Sony wide screen TV to know what was going on?

HE listened and heard her pain. He had heard her suffering for more than five hundred eighty-five years, give or take a few. It was not the first time he acknowledged he was less than perfect.

That was not something he wanted spread around.

I SCREWED UP. WHAT CAN I SAY? I USUALLY DO NOT SUCUMB TO PRESSURE BUT THE CRUSADES, THE MIDDLE AGES, WAS NOT AN EASY GIG FOR ME. FOR ANY OF US. HOW DO I MAKE IT UP TO A UNFULLFILLED NINETEEN YEAR OLD? WHAT CAN I DO FOR HER AND WHY HAVE I WAITED SO LONG?

He sat by himself and pondered.

THE ETERNAL SHTUP

HE was well aware of the saying, 'Better late than never'. UP HERE there is no never. HE knew in HIS heart he had to do something. But what? Few people knew that Jeanne was so busy listening to the voices, to trying to save her country, to being ridiculed by everyone at every turn; that she had no time to socialize. She had never had a boyfriend or a real honest to HIM date.

Known only to HIM, she had died a virgin.

THAT'S IT. THAT'S HOW I'LL TRY AND MAKE IT UP TO HER. BUT WITH WHO?

HE had thousands, actually millions to choose from. Great military leaders, heads of state, movie stars, politicians, musicians, you name it. The list was endless. It had to be someone young enough for Joan to relate to, someone she could admire, someone who would understand her suffering.

HE, with HIS vast powers did not need a list from Google of all those under thirty five, that would fit the bill. HE knew it had to be someone special.

HE sat alone on a distant cloud so as not to be disturbed. Finally, like a bolt of lightning, it hit him. It almost knocked him off HIS ass.

O M M. OH MY ME.

HE wondered if it would be sacrilegious to even suggest it to Joanie. HE wondered how she would react. HE knew they did in fact have a great deal in common. They both died for what they truly believed in. In a sense, they were both holy martyrs.

That was a big plus.

I'LL DO IT. I'LL LET THE CHIPS FALL WHERE THEY MAY. THE DECISION IS MINE TO MAKE AND I'VE JUST MADE IT.

HE understood this could not be coincidental. It could not be a chance meeting in front of the library. Not on line at Starbucks, if there were a Starbucks. Both parties had to know HE had carefully arranged this.

Separately he invited both of them to a distant cloud. In an instant, or was it a minute, not that it made any different, they both appeared.

HE held his breath.

"I ASSUME I DO NOT HAVE TO INTRODUCE BOTH OF YOU TO EACH OTHER. THIS IS NOT A COINCIDENCE. NOR IS THIS IS A HOOKUP. IT IS MY WAY OF UNDOING WHAT HAS ALREADY BEEN DONE. IT IS MY WILL THAT YOU AT LEAST BE FRIENDLY AND AT LEAST GIVE IT A CHANCE."

They each looked at each other wondering if this was some type of cruel joke.

"I DO NOT PLAY GAMES. IT IS WHAT IT APPEARS TO BE. TRUST ME ON THAT ONE."

They both looked at HIM. They again looked at each other.

THE ETERNAL SHTUP

"Why she's Joan of Arc."

"My God, I think he's Jesus Christ."

She was not quite sure.

"YES HE IS. HE'S MY SON. MY ONLY BEGOTTEN SON."

Both stared. Neither moved a muscle. It was not clear either actually had muscles.

Jesus' first thought was, Mary Magdalena.

"IT'S O.K. I KNOW WHAT I'M DOING. SHE'LL UNDERSTAND. I PROMISE YOU."

Jesus was not so sure. It had been just over two thousand years and not a single day had gone by when he did not think of her.

PLEASE DO ME A BIG FAVOR. AT LEAST TALK. GIVE IT A CHANCE. I'LL BE BY LATER."

A second later, HE was gone. They were now alone. With each other.

She was burned at the stake. Actually tied to a stone pillar. He was crucified, on a dogwood tree. Already they had something in common.

"It was HIS suggestion, not mine. I guess the least we can do is walk and talk. What harm would it do?"

Joanie smiled.

Without that scruffy beard, with his hair now properly shampooed, cut and styled, with that tailored white with gold trimmed, above the knee, tunic and designer sandals, he's a looker. He could be a keeper.

The late, great, J.C., as some had called him, was also thinking.

She looks awfully young but has that look of determination in her eyes. She's no floozy. Maybe HE is on the right track. It's about time I had a little fun. It's not easy being who I am. Whenever anyone stubs their toe or hits their finger with a hammer, they call out my name. It's like they don't realize I too can hear them.

Jesus then thought, *I'm never invited to all the 'really good' parties.*

Without giving it another thought, he took her hand in his, and decided to go for a walk. They were in no hurry. They had all day. They really had forever.

36

People talk. People gossip. It is the nature of the beast. But when the gossip involves Jesus Christ and Joan of Arc, and the intervening force is HIM, it is more than just gossip.

The real question was, was it physical or cerebral? An intellectual meeting or an everyday hook up?

People believed what they wanted to believe. Besides, there were too many cerebral relationships already to talk about. Plato and Aristotle met every morning before the library opened; some claimed it never closed, to discuss who knows what. You would think after two thousand three hundred and some sixty four years, they would run out of conversation or arguments. No such problems with J.C. as his apostle buddies called him and Joanie, that J.C. had now nicknamed her.

For two lonely people who had both been in the same place for more than five hundred years together, they had a lot of catching up to do. As outspoken as he was as an advocate on Earth, Jesus became somewhat of a recluse UP HERE.

I hate it when people play favorites. I did not ask to be HIS son. I was happy to be a Jewish carpenter. Had I not been consumed with HIM, and having Peter, Paul and Mary, oops, Judas always telling me what to do and where to be, I would have found a nice Jewish girl and started a family. I would have had a son, HE willing, who would be Bar Mitzvah.

NO YOU WOULD NOT. I MAKE THE RULES, YOU WERE SUPPOSE TO IMPLIMENT THEM. KAPISH? SORRY IT DIDN'T WORK OUT AS I HAD PLANNED. THOSE DAMN ROMANS.

HE rarely cursed.

Jesus had always been taught to respect his elders, listen to his father, especially when his father was HIM.

He remembered he had promised Joanie he would take her to the Lincoln / Douglas debates. You would think after more than seven debates, a few thousand dress rehearsals over one hundred sixty years ago, there would be little to talk about.

Joanie was wearing a new soft cotton toga. It was fitted at the waist, had a more revealing scoop neckline and clung to her chest. She too had her hair styled in a most striking manner.

She looks hot.

It was the second or third or tenth time he thought that.

HE knew exactly what his son was thinking.

THE ETERNAL SHTUP

GO FOR IT. WHAT DO YOU HAVE TO LOSE? I KNOW YOU HAVE WAITED LONG ENOUGH AND DESERVE IT.

Everyone heard HIM. Only Jesus knew who HE was talking to.

It's good to know I now have HIS permission. The question is, am I ready? Is she ready?

YOU'RE MORE THAN TWO THOUSAND YEARS OLD. SHE'S OVER FIVE HUNDRED YEARS OLD. IF NOT NOW, WHEN?

"Ready?"

"I've been ready for the last five hundred eighty eight years."

Jesus blushed. "I meant, to go to the debate."

After all those years, you would think the philosophy of Abe the politician, and Stephen Douglas the Senator, would be different. It wasn't. J.C and Joanie left early. Everyone knew the results. The next thing they both knew, they were on a distant cloud. It was bright and sunny, as usual, and not another soul in sight.

It's now or never, he thought.

I hope he's gentle. It's my first time, Joanie prayed.

DON'T WORRY. IT'LL BE GOOD FOR BOTH OF YOU. TRUST ME.

Neither had much of a choice.

Afterwards he asked, "Do you happen to have a cigarette on you?"

Joan, who had looked most satisfied, now had a look of horror on her face.

"I don't smoke. I don't carry matches and I've been scared to death of fire for the past five hundred years."

Jesus quickly remembered and apologized.

HE had witnessed the whole thing. And why not, J.C. was HIS son. HIS only son. It was HIS right. Some would say, HIS G-d given right.

SHTUPPING IS GOOD. MORRIS WAS RIGHT. SHTUPPING IS VERY GOOD.

37

Morris had not played golf or taken a lesson in some time. He could not get used to the concept of time or more precisely, lack of it. Did a round of eighteen holes take three hours or six or thirty minutes. The balls never seemed to land out of bounds, the traps were always cleaned and easy to pitch out of and the greens true. No one ever lost.

And then there was Tiffany.

He wondered if Bobby would mind if he hung around Tiff now that he was always sniffing around Marilyn. He assumed Veronica would. The problem was his thinking. Everyone knew what everyone else was thinking and every time he saw or thought of Tiffany, he thought of one thing and one thing only.

Schtupping.

How could he not.

Morris now had a moral dilemma. He was surrounded by some of the greatest minds in history, all for the asking and he was afraid to ask.

Anyone.

He was sure Tiffany would not say no. it was no crime or sin, besides she loved it and was the best there was. Would she tell Veronica? What was there to gain? What would Veronica say or do? Would Veronica cut him off? He prayed not. So why risk it? A question posed by some of the most successful men in history, from biblical characters who were always begotten someone else's wife, to Lords and Kings, to presidents and world leaders, and none of them could keep it in their pants for very long.

It was an occupational hazard. Just ask LBJ, or Ike or Slick Willie and sure as hell, Donald. Everybody in the world knew about Jack. If you had a penis, you felt a need to share it. Preferably with any female, young or old, black or white, short or tall, who would allow you to. What was wrong with that? The penis had a head; it obviously had a mind of its own also.

It did not like rejection. It was a selfish and ever needy organ.

Morris reasoned if he could not control it, he could not be held responsible for what it did. That was all the rationale he needed. He thought about the driving range – and Tiffany – and no sooner could he yell, "Fore" and he was there.

It took Tiff a good five seconds to read his mind.

THE ETERNAL SHTUP

"Why not. And trust me; I won't mention this to anyone, especially Veronica. It," and here she smiled, "will stay between the two of us. For as long as you want."

Morris understood.

Had he still been alive, no question he would have had a premature ejaculation. She was that desirable. But now he was UP HERE and the possibility never occurred to him. The Kama Sutra had nothing on Tiffany. She knew every trick in the book and some the book had never thought of. She was wise and patient. She was caring and understanding. And most of all, she was willing.

Morris would have thought he had died and gone to UP HERE, except he was already dead and he was already UP HERE.

"It can never be any better than that. It was fantastic. You are fantastic."

"Wait. There is always more; there is always better. You just gotta believe."

Morris closed his eyes and silently thanked HIM.

"YOU'RE WELCOME MORRIS. YOU WILL ENJOY YOURSELF MUCH MORE UP HERE BY THINKING ABOUT PLEASING YOURSELF, NOT ME. I CAN HANDLE MY OWN PROBLEMS."

HE was immediately sorry he used the word, "problems."

Morris got the message, loud and clear. He looked at Tiffany again. She still had not put her toga back on yet.

"Again?"

Morris had that pleading look in his eyes. He was also still hard.

"As long as you're up to it, why not."

He did not have to thank HIM again. HE knew it.

"How was your golf game, Morris?"

He could not lie, even if he wanted to. His face turned beet red.

Veronica waited. She knew. She just had to look at his face.

"I didn't play golf, I didn't take a lesson. At least not that sort of a lesson. I had sex with Tiffany."

"Was it good?"

Morris had no idea what to say. If he was honest Veronica would never talk to him again. If he lied, she would know it. He was caught between two very unappealing choices.

He knew it. She knew it.

THE ETERNAL SHTUP

"Yes, I guess it was good. Tiffany has a great deal of experience. But she does not know me like you know me. She probably has had too many lovers in her lifetime. She is not very discriminate. Not like you."

"Anything you care to teach me?"

Morris knew he was off the hook. At least for a while.

HE was listening. And possibly learning.

"Of course," Morris answered.

All's well that ends well. So far.

"Men are like putty. All you have to know is how and where to twist them. It's not even a contest anymore."

Tiffany thought back to a few hours ago and what was happening with Morris and Veronica right now. She could have predicted it; chapter, line and verse. It was no big deal, to anyone. You are here to enjoy yourself and whether it is golf or tennis, shuffleboard or schtupping, it makes no difference. As long as it gives one pleasure.

Tiffany had been giving and receiving pleasure for more than one hundred fifty years. Why Bobby Kennedy was a mere newbie as far as she was concerned. She thought back to some of the dukes and royalty in France in the 1800's. They were some first class studs and she bedded them all. Well not every single one of them, but her dance card was always full. She was in demand. All because she listened to what they wanted and gave them what they needed.

Economics 101 – Supply and Demand. She had it, they wanted it. All that was necessary to complete the deal was a *quid pro quo*. Cash for services rendered. In Tiffany's case, she never accepted cash. She wanted favors. Favors could buy her far more than cash ever could and was much more delicious.

It didn't take a Louis XIV to figure that formula out.

Today Tiffany wanted nothing for her favors. She had it all, and then some. She was happy she could deliver the goods – on demand.

HE was pleased. HE had done his job.

AND DID IT WELL, I MIGHT ADD.

38

MY TURN.

It seemed like a constant refrain. Like a song that get stuck in your brain and no matter what else you are thinking, you are constantly humming it. Like *Fiddler on the Roof*.

If I were a rich man, yadda, dada, dada . . .

DOES IT REALLY HAVE TO BE MY TURN? ALL THESES CENTURIES I HAVE MANAGED QUITE NICELY ALONE, THANK YOU. NOW EVERYONE IS A JEWISH MATCHMAKER.

He knew it would be nice to talk to someone at the end of the day. The problem was, the day never ended. When it was nighttime in New York, it was the next morning in Sydney. If HE took forty winks at midnight in Manhattan, he would not hear the pleas of those in Australia who had their own problems tomorrow.

"Do you have a minute, SIR?"

"BUT OF COURSE. FOR YOU I HAVE MAYBE TWO MINUTES."

HE was joking; HE already knew why Veronica had come to him. For advice. If he charged one half of what the shrinks were getting, he would have as much money as, well as much as most people thought HE had.

"I ASSUME IT'S ABOUT MORRIS AND TIFFANY. SHE DOES GET AROUND, DOESN'T SHE? MAY I ASK YOU A PERSONAL QUESTION?"

HE knows everything. Why would HE even bother to ask?

"Of course."

"DOES HE KEEP YOU HAPPY. SATISFIED. CONTENT. YOU KNOW WHAT I MEAN. DO YOU WANT TO BE WITH HIM?"

"Of course."

"SO WHAT'S THE PROBLEM?"

Veronica paused. What was the problem? All of a sudden it seemed so minor. Morris was hurting no one. His appetite was a little bigger than most. It was not as if he was cheating, they were never married and he did not lie when asked about Tiffany. And most important, as she told HIM, she was happy, content and satisfied. What more could she ask for?

Nothing.

THE ETERNAL SHTUP

"HAVE A SUPERCALIFRAGLICTIC DAY VERONICA. AND TELL MORRIS TO KEEP UP THE GOOO WORK."

Veronica gave him a look. She was not sure how he meant it.

"Thank you SIR."

HE was hoping word would get out as to his remarks and maybe some unhappy wives would have a few more dollars in their pockets and their sleazy divorce lawyers would handle more civil rights and *pro bono* cases.

ONE CAN ONLY HOPE. ONE CAN TRULY HOPE.

There appeared to be a commotion on the steps of the library. A crowd was gathering and HE could see placards. Another unauthorized demonstration.

JUST WHAT I NEED RIGHT NOW.

On the top step, as usual, was Gandhi. He said nothing. He did not have to. Just his presence at the rally caused a degree of legitimacy. He attended few such rallies, but when he did, people gathered and listened.

HE decided to stay in the background and find out what the frustrated lawyer, a nonviolent civil disobedient if there ever was one, was up to this time. There were no problems UP HERE that HE was aware of.

The truth was, this was not Mahatma's fight. He was merely a front man for someone else. The question was who and why. HE did not like surprises, HE did not like disobedience, civil or otherwise, and he certainly did not like unannounced and clearly unauthorized rallies.

HE was about to find out what was going on, and why, when he was distracted by one of the loveliest lady he had ever seen, who walked by. She flickered her eye lashes and lowered her eyes in a most flirtatious way. The only word HE could think of was exotic. Her neck was long and jewels adorned her head. She could have been a queen.

In fact she was.

HE was immediately struck by her charm, beauty and cautiousness. She did not stop or say hello but merely continued on her merry way. HE was sure if she had a dainty hanky, she would have politely dropped it. It would have been a race to see who picked it up. HE was sure she was used to a hundred servants following her, willing to lay down their very life for her. And it would have been anticipated.

HE had to know who she was.

It then came to HIM.

OF COURSE, HOW COULD I HAVE POSSIBLY FORGOTTEN. I HAVE NOT SEEN HER IN A THOUSAND YEARS, MAYBE MORE.

HE had heard rumors, her hairdo, bejeweled with precious stones, was really a million dollar wig.

THE ETERNAL SHTUP

She actually had been UP HERE for more than thirty three hundred years, her date of entry in the Good Book was given as one thousand three hundred thirty, B.C. HE quickly recalled her husband had been Akhenaton, the Egyptian Pharaoh. Of the many names given to her, Queen of Egypt, Lady of Grace, Lady of All Women and the Great King's Wife, made her feel best.

HE wanted to call out, Nefertiti, please don't rush off. It's such a beautiful day; perhaps we could find ourselves a quiet cloud so we could talk. Before he could utter a word, she was gone.

HE looked everywhere. She was not to be found.

I WILL FIND HER. THAT YOU CAN BE SURE OF.

HE looked down and there was Morris, perhaps the last person he wanted to see

or talk to.

"Sir, she just entered the Hall of the Ancient Heroes. She goes there every afternoon to 'talk' to her late husband."

HOW DOES HE KNOW WHO I AM LOOKING FOR?

"THANK YOU MORRIS. IF YOU WILL NOW EXCUSE ME."

Sure enough, Nefertiti was sitting on an old stone bench in front of great granite statues HE agreed to have put up more than twenty five hundred years ago.

Long before the coming of Jesus.

It helped appease some of the old timers.

HE felt it would be impolite to interrupt. She was talking to one of the statues. It was a one sided conversation.

No question she missed him. HE wondered why Akhenaton was not UP HERE also. He would ask Peter when he had a chance. HE also wondered how Morris knew so much. HE didn't like it. Not for one minute, however long that was.

IF SHE IS STILL PINING AFTER THREE THOUSAND YEARS, SHE WOULD NOT MAKE A GOOD PARTNER FOR ME. BESIDES, TOO MUCH JEWELRY, TOO MUCH MAKEUP, TOO MUCH POMP AND CIRCUMSTANCE. OH WELL.

HE was seriously thinking of giving up the search. It was too emotionally draining, regardless of the pool of talent available to HIM

Morris was coincidentally hanging around to see if HE would make a move on Nefertiti. He bet yes. He was wrong.

"IS THERE SOMETHING I CAN DO FOR YOU MORRIS, IS EVERYTHING ALRIGHT WITH VERONICA AND YOU? YOU SEEM TO BE FOLLOWING ME AROUND A LOT LATELY. AM I MISTAKEN?"

Morris did not know what to say. He was even afraid to think.

THE ETERNAL SHTUP

"You'll excuse me SIR. I have to be somewhere else right now."

With that, Morris was gone. HE knew Morris had nowhere else to go.

TOO BAD NEFERTITI WE COULD HAVE BEEN A GREAT COUPLE. YOU HAD ALL KINDS OF EXPERIECE BEING A QUEEN AND KNOWING THE DEMANDS OF BEING WITH A KING. OH WELL, MAYBE IN A THOUSAND YEARS FROM NOW.

Morris was back in his little cottage with Veronica. He was afraid to go out; he was afraid HE was listening or watching. He knew he overstepped his bounds. No sense screwing up a good thing. Speaking of screwing up a good thing, his thoughts went back to Tiffany. He looked down to see it begin to grow.

Morris began to hum, *Miracle of miracles, Miracle of miracle. Of all G-d's miracles, G-d made you.*

He then thought, *Should I, shouldn't I? Do I, don't I?*

"DON'T PUSH YOUR LUCK MORRIS."

Morris' decision had been made for him.

He hesitated for a minute – and only a minute.

"Veronica, how would you like to make love - now?"

No sense wasting a good erection, Morris thought.

"Of course Morris. Whatever you want."

Her remark merely reaffirmed what he had known for some time.

There is a heaven, there is a G-d.

39

It was time. Actually it was long past due. A decision had finally been made. Now HE would share it - with all. The WORD would go forth from this day forward. All in Heaven and on Earth would now know.

The sun shone bright, the birds were quiet, the winds slowed to a mere rustle. All the inhabitants put down whatever they were doing. They all stood respectfully to listen to what HE had to say.

"I HAVE NO NEED TO HAVE CHILDREN, MORE CHILDREN. YOU ARE ALL MY CHILDREN. I LOVE YOU ALL. YOU KNOWN THAT. YOU ALSO KNOW THAT RECENTLY I HAVE SPENT SOME TIME THINKING ABOUT MY OWN WELL BEING. MAKING SURE I WAS COMPLETELY HAPPY. CONTENT MIGHT BE A BETTER WORD. I HAVE SPENT TIME GETTING TO KNOW MORE THAN A FEW WONDERFUL WOMEN UP HERE. I HAVE MADE NO SECRET ABOUT IT. IT HAS BEEN OPEN AND BEYOND APPROACH. THERE ARE THOUSANDS MORE I COULD HAVE BEEN WITH. ACTUALLY HUNDREDS OF THOUSANDS, BUT WHO'S COUNTING. IT WOULD NOT HAVE

MADE ANY DIFFERENCE IN THE FINAL OUTCOME. I THANK THEM ALL FOR THEIR PATIENCE AND UNDERSTANDING. IT WAS A DIFFICULT PROCESS FOR ALL. VERY RECENTLY I HAVE MADE A DECISION."

HE looked over his vast kingdom not knowing how they would react. The crowd was fidgety as might be expected.

"FIRST, I FEEL I WOULD LIKE, I DID NOT SAY NEED, I SAID LIKE, A CONFIDENTE. SOMEONE TO TALK TO AFTER A LONG DAY OF LISTENING TO THE PROBLEMS OF THE WORLD. YOU HAVE NO IDEA HOW DRAINING IT REALLY IS. SECOND, I TOO WOULD LIKE TO KICK BACK AT TIMES AND NOT BE WHO I AM. I LOVE ME AND ENJOY BEING ME, BUT FOR A FEW HOURS I WOULD JUST AS SOON PREFER TO BE YOU."

Here there was a pause. The sound of a pin could be heard, if someone had actually dropped one.

"ALL MY DECISIONS ARE FINAL. THERE ARE NO APPEALS. AT TIMES I FEEL IT WOULD BE MORE JUDICIOUS IF I HAD SOMEONE TO USE AS A SOUNDING BOARD. TO LISTEN TO MY REASONING, FAULTLESS AS IT IS, AS A WAY OF REASSURING ME I HAVE MADE THE RIGHT CHOICE. THIS IS NOT SECOND GUESSING, MERELY TESTING WHAT I ALREADY KNOW TO BE TRUE. FOR THAT I NEED A PARTNER, ONE WHO I TRUST IMPLICITLY, ONE WHO I WOULD LISTEN TO WITH THE SAME RESPECT THAT MY PARTNER WOULD LISTEN TO ME."

The names of those now in contention switched from the most beautiful, the most sensual, the most alluring, to the brightest, most intellectual, the keenest minds in the kingdom. Speculation was rampant as to who HE had in mind. Maybe someone both beautiful and smart.

Before a list of names and faces could be conjured up, HE raised both hands. They held their collective breaths, waiting.

HE had an enormous smile on his face as he continued to speak.

"IT WAS NOT WITHOUT A GREAT DEAL OF SELF EXAMINATION AND PRAYER THAT I CAME TO MY DECISION."

Here he paused to reflect, for one last time.

"MY NEW LIFE PARTNER IS KAROL JOZEF WOJTYLA.

Again, dead silence. One could almost hear the brains swirling. The processing began.

Who was Karol Wojtyla and why was her name so familiar.

Then it came to them - in unison. Karol Wojtyla was a he, not a she, he being the former Arch Bishop of Krakow, then Cardinal Wojtyla and his final earthly name, Pope John Paul II.

Now Saint John Paul II.

HE had chosen a man. A Man of G-d. One of the most loved, adored, beautiful and obviously brightest man to ever serve as Pope of the Catholic Church.

It took a few minutes to understand but the crowd, everyone, stood and cheered. They laughed and cried, they yelled and clapped, they were overjoyed in HIS choice. It could not have been better, in Heaven or on Earth.

No one cheered louder or was more pleased than Morris. He was sure that although HE now had a partner, he and God would still be BFF.

Morris smiled. He was happy for his best friend and he wanted everyone to know it.

Maybe HE needs a nice engagement ring. I could get it for him, wholesale. No commission. None. Zilch.

HE heard the thought and decided not to comment. Definitely not his *shtick*. HE too was pleased. Pleased that others saw what he saw, pleased with what he had done, it was indeed the perfect choice for a perfect partner.

To serve him for a lifetime Is more than any one man could ever hope for. To have my contemporaries elect me pope was the crowning achievement of a lifetime for anyone. To be HIS partner eternally Is too much to comprehend.

Karol, he seldom thought of himself as John Paul or Pope John Paul II and never, never as Saint John Paul the Great, sat back and reflected. He was born in a small town in Poland in 1920. By the time he was twenty one he had lost his mother, father, older brother and sister. He moved to Krakow and considered the priesthood.

THE ETERNAL SHTUP

I still remember the only "love affair" I ever had. Ginka Beer was Jewish with stupendous dark eyes and jet black hair. She was absolutely beautiful. What if, what if?

I was Pope for twenty seven years and believe I achieved my fondest wish; creating a new religious alliance that brought together Jews, Muslims and Christians. Not bad for a little Polish kid from the sticks.

Karol sat on a small, fluffy cloud alone and reflected on his past life. He had done good. He had done bags and bags of good. Now he would be HIS eternal companion.

John Paul had a glow about him. And why shouldn't he?

He could just picture some truly audacious conversations with HIM.

Epilouge

In heaven, five years seemed like five minutes; five minutes seemed like five years. There was no way of telling the difference. It obviously made no difference.

No one was going anywhere.

Flash forward.

Morris almost did not recognize Esther. She looked twenty-five, not the seventy year old who thought the oven in the kitchen was a good place to store old files. Esther, his wife who he had last seen on his death bed was now UP HERE. She knew of course all about Morris and Veronica. She also knew about Consuelo the cleaning lady and all those that followed her. There were too many to count and the fact was, the more time he spent with his bimbos, the less effort she was required to spend with him on the weekends.

Doesn't he know you don't do those things at our age?

Esther had led a comfortable, if not a particularly exciting life. There were the seven day long Caribbean cruises during the winter and a few weeks in Miami with so called friends in the summer. All in all, she had no regrets.

Veronica purposely stood in the background as Morris asked his wife, they had never been divorced, how the boys were doing. Naturally Max had taken over the family business but it had not been the same since he passed. Max was now in the process of liquidating. All Benny wanted to know was, "How much?" He had a big deal right around the corner and needed some quick seed money.

Max claimed the old velvet pouch had less than a dozen stones in it. Not great quality. Morris knew better. There were at least fifty five. All VVS.

"So nothing has changed Esther?"

"No Morris, nothing."

She looked over at Veronica slowly, from top to bottom.

"I see you're again with a *shicksa*."

"We're UP HERE. What's the difference what her religion was Down There?"

"Maybe I'll see you around Morris. Maybe I won't. Have a nice day Veronica."

With that she sashayed off. She was dying to look back.

She didn't.

RFK could not have been more pleased. He was now his own man. He was recognized for who he was and what he did, not who he was related to. Joe Sr. was not particularly happy. Rose Kennedy was delighted. She had not talked to her late husband since the day before he died. On Earth he had been a tyrant. He never asked, he demanded. Here, he was a nobody. Maybe not quite a nobody but the father of a president and attorney general that had both been assassinated.

Bobby was in constant demand as the premier Ambassador of Love. He would have loved to spend more time, professionally and privately with Marilyn, but it was not to be. HE felt it was in Bobby's best interests to do what he did best. And that would be talking and convincing large groups that HIS way was the best way. As to his other talents, there were others with far more experience.

Tiffany moved back home. Actually she moved from one cloud to another. Back to Section A. If HE had chosen another woman over her, after all she had taught him, all she had given of herself; it would have been tough to ever look HIM in the eyes again. But HE didn't. HE chose another man. One who had been celibate his entire life.

Well at least since he became a parish priest.

This is a whole new ballgame. How can I be jealous of the Pope?

A man of the cloth, someone who had never known the unbelievable joys and satisfaction of a sensuous and truly liberated woman.

She couldn't. She knew it and HE knew it.

John Paul still had the glow about him. It radiated for miles and miles. No one really knew what a mile was. He was seen smiling and talking to everyone – about everything. The phrase often came to him, THE RIGHT HAND OF GOD.

That would be me, he thought.

YES IT WOULD. YES IT WOULD.

HE had a habit of repeating himself.

They both laughed about it, but not too loud. No sense in sharing an inside joke with everyone.

There was very little verbal communication between the two of them. Each knew what the other was thinking, at times before it was even thought. John Paul would begin a thought and HE would finish it. It was a big time-saver, not that time was such an important commodity UP HERE.

They agreed on virtually everything. When they didn't, they listened to the other's arguments. If they still did not agree they had more experts, on every subject imaginable, then any other location, anywhere. It was like having the Congressional Library of Congress, The Louvre, the

THE ETERNAL SHTUP

Smithsonian and everything on Google, all wrapped into one tight ball.

HE sat back and thought about Morris. Morris and his constant need for schtupping. In all HIS years, way too many to count, he had never run into anyone quite like Morris. Maybe it was now time to sit down and have a heart-to-heart with him. There was a distinct possibility they both had something to learn.

"MORRIS, IF YOU COULD SPARE A FEW MOMENTS,"

What have I done this time, Morris wondered.

DO I REALLY NEED TO TELL YOU, MORRIS?

They both knew it would not be their last audacious conversation with each other. They had all the time in the universe.

"I'll be there in a minute SIR. I just have something I must finish."

"SORRY I INTERRUPTED."

Morris smiled at Veronica who was still lying in bed. Anxiously waiting.

SOME THINGS NEVER CHANGE.

ROY SANDERS

###

IF YOU ENJOYED, UNDERSTOOD, TOLERATED

OR WERE EMBARRSSED BY

THE ETERNAL SHTUP,

THE AUTHOR HIGLY RECOMMENDS HIS LATEST EFFORT

*

GOD ONLY KNOWS

*

Another Heavenly Comedy

God Only Knows, Copyright 2017, Roy Sanders, All Rights Reserved

1.

Life could not be sweeter. And why shouldn't it be.

They were the perfect couple. Karol Jozef Wojtyla, the former Arch Bishop of Krakow, then Cardinal Wojtyla and his final earthly name, Pope John Paul II, now Saint John Paul and HIM, Ruler of the Entire Universe, were partners, soul mates, companions and BFF, best friends forever.

TRUST ME, FOREVER ACTUALLY MEANS FOREVER.

THE ETERNAL SHTUP

They did not fight, they did not argue and there were few topics they were not well versed in. With all the choices available to HIM, and HE had the cream of the crop, HE had gone for wisdom, companionship and to somewhat lesser degree, equality.

Physical beauty was too overrated, at times too shallow.

Morris would have argued, not that it would have done him any good. He never claimed to be a scholar. His limited expertise was in a far different area. One that HE nor Karol had absolutely any interest in.

Shtupping. Constant, eternal shtupping. As in non-stop fornication.

HE knew he could not please everyone. Not so much ladies like Nefertiti, Cleopatra, Helen of Troy, Marilyn, or even Jane Russell, but the myriad of former popes who felt more than slighted.

The list was practically endless. From Benedict XVI, 2005 till he unexpectedly resigned in 2013; to Urban II who lead the First Crusade, 1042 – 1099, when 100,000 followers marched on Jerusalem; to Pius XII, 1939-1958, the period of his highly critical rein during World War II; to St. Peter, one of the twelve Apostles; to Gregory IX who instituted the Papal Inquisition.

The universal complaint, thou never spoken too loudly, was:

Why him. Why not me?

John Paul felt St. Peter, Urban II and Gregory IX had legitimate arguments. As to HIM, no explanation was needed.

WHO DO THEY THINK APPOINTED THEM IN THE FIRST PLACE? THE COLLEGE OF CARDINALS? AND WHO CAME UP WITH THAT CONCEPT. ME, OF COURSE.

The discussion was now closed. Forever.

Morris had mixed feeling.

I have been HIS BFF. We sorta hung out together. HE was always available, no matter what my problem was. Even my insatiable appetite for schtupping. Bless HIM, he understood my human frailties.

Morris now wondered if HE would still have the time for him.

"NOT TO WORRY MORRIS. I NEVER FORGET MY FRIENDS. WHY WITHOUT YOU, IT WOULD HAVE TAKEN ME A BIT LONGER TO COME UP WITH USING ESOTERIC SEX TO CURB EARTH'S POPULATION AND THE AMBASSADORS OF LOVE IDEA."

I thought it was Tiffany who came up with Esoteric Sex?

"YOU THOUGHT WRONG MORRIS. WHO DO YOU THINK CAME UP WITH THE CONCEPT IN THE FIRST PLACE. TIFF MERELY REMEMBERED WHAT TREVANIAN WROTE. IT WAS MY IDEA. BEST YOU DON'T FORGET IT."

THE ETERNAL SHTUP

"Yes SIR. Obviously I was wrong."

"YES YOU WERE. NOT TO WORRY, YOU ARE FORGIVEN, MORRIS."

"Who were you just talking to?"

Karol was having some difficulty when talking to his new partner / companion / mate.

Do I call HIM Abe, a nickname he always liked; Sir, Your Holiness, G-d or just begin a conversation without a salutation?

"WHATEVER MAKES YOU MOST COMFORTABLE, KAROL."

"Ah, thanks, Abe."

"SEE, THAT WAS NOT SO DIFFICULT, WAS IT?"

Karol didn't answer. He didn't have to.

HE knows what I'm thinking, usually before I think it.

YOU'RE RIGHT AS RAIN, ON THE WINDOW PANE, KAY.

HE decided when they were alone; he would call his new roommate, Kay, short for Karol.

IT HAS A NICE RING TO IT.

"So, what's your schedule like today," Kay asked.

"TODAY, TOMORROW, YESTERDAY. ALWAYS THE SAME. PROBLEMS. AM I THE ONLY ONE WITH ANSWERS? OH, IT WAS MORRIS WHO ASKED ME A QUESTION. YOU'LL MEET HIM SOON. YOU'LL LOVE HIM. A BIT PECULIAR. ALL HE WANTS TO DO IS SHTUP. ALL DAY LONG. HE'LL HURT HIMSELF IF HE KEEPS THIS UP."

Karol said nothing. It didn't seem right. A waste of good energy. He was still not sure how far he was allowed to go with criticism. The 'relationship' was still in the 'honeymoon' stage.

"It's your gig. You asked for it. No one is about to be sorry for YOU."

"YOU GOT ME THERE BIG BOY."

You could almost cut the tension with a dull kitchen knife. While everyone UP HERE, was thrilled, this had been a whole new experience for all of them. Would it last? Was it right? Did HE really need a best buddy? What did they do, what did they talk about, when they were alone?

"IT'S REALLY NONE OF YOUR BUSINESS."

When HE made the announcement, there was a roar that could be heard from one giant cloud to another. The celebration was nonstop. After what seemed like Mardi Gras, Chinese New Year and Rio's Carnival, all rolled into one, HE

THE ETERNAL SHTUP

felt enough was enough. HE also noticed Karol was not in a celebratory mood.

"WHAT'S BOTHERING YOU BUBBY?"

He loved to use Yiddish expressions when he could get away with it. The Jews claimed they were the chosen people. They weren't, but HE didn't have the *chutzpa* to tell them.

YOU KNOW I PLAY NO FAVORITES. I JUST LIKE ALL THOSE WEIRD YIDDISH EXPRESSIONS.

Karol had a problem. He was afraid to tell HIM. He was also afraid to think it. HE could read everyone's every thought.

For millions and millions of year, since HE created all this, HE has been alone. He had no mate, no companion, no BFF. So why now? Why me? We are not equals, not by a long shot. While DOWN THERE, I was his servant. I did HIS bidding. I served HIM in the only way I knew how. So now how can we be partners? When will HE get tired of me? What happens when I get a "Dear Karol, letter?

"STOP WORRYING BUBELEH, WHEN I SAY FOREVER IS FOREVER, I MEAN IT."

Karol smiled.

What else can I do?

*

SO WHAT HAPPENS – STAY TUNED. BUY THE BOOK
THANKS,
ROY

*

PS. IN THE EVENT YOU DID NOT LIKE THIS BOOK AND MAY NOT LIKE THE NEXT, I AM OFFERING A 100% RETURN OF MONEY, POSTAGE, GAS MILAGE AND ANY OTHER EXPENSES INCURRED. You Know Who.
NOTE
THE AUTHOR, THE DISTRIBUTOR, THE PUBLISHER, DISCLAIM ANY REPRESENTATIONS "HE" HAS MADE. TRUST BUT VERIFY.

www.ingramcontent.com/pod-product-compliance
Lightning Source LLC
Chambersburg PA
CBHW021423070526
44577CB00001B/29